PHILIP TOWLE

Hampton
New Hampshire

HIS ENGLISH ORIGINS
AND
SOME AMERICAN
DESCENDANTS

William Haslet Jones

HERITAGE BOOKS
2012

HERITAGE BOOKS

AN IMPRINT OF HERITAGE BOOKS, INC.

Books, CDs, and more—Worldwide

For our listing of thousands of titles see our website
at
www.HeritageBooks.com

Published 2012 by
HERITAGE BOOKS, INC.
Publishing Division
100 Railroad Ave. #104
Westminster, Maryland 21157

Other Heritage Books by the author:

CD: *Genealogies, Volume 6: The William Haslet Jones Collection*

*Philip Towle, Hampton, New Hampshire: His English Origins
and Some American Descendants*

*The Rowell Family of New England and Their English Origins, 1560–1900:
Descendants of Thomas Rowell 1594–1662*

Vital Statistics of Chichester, New Hampshire, 1742–1927

Vital Statistics of Epsom, New Hampshire, 1727–1927

Vital Statistics of Seabrook, New Hampshire, 1768–1903

William Tilton: His English Origins and Some American Descendants

*Winkley Family: The English Origin of Captain Samuel Winkley
and Some New England Descendants*

International Standard Book Numbers
Paperbound: 978-0-7884-0190-9
Clothbound: 978-0-7884-9119-1

PHILIP TOWLE, HAMPTON, N.H.

TABLE OF CONTENTS

PHILIP TOWLE, HAMPTON, N.H.

INTRODUCTION

Among the early settlers of Hampton, N.H. was a Philip Towle. He married ISABELLA AUSTIN there in 1657. The Philip Towle family history in New England was presented by Mrs. A. Lindsey in the NEHGR in 1889, v.43, pg 364. The GENEALOGICAL DICTIONARY OF MAINE & NEW HAMPSHIRE, by Sybil Noyes, etal, Portland, Me. 1928-1939 covers the Towle family of Hampton. Other sources of information on the New England Towles include Joseph Dow, HISTORY OF THE TOWN OF HAMPTON, N.H., Salem, Mass. 1893 and Langdon B. Parson, HISTORY OF THE TOWN OF RYE, N.H., Concord, N.H. 1905. At the Newberry Library, Chicago, Illinois there is a large manuscript collection accumulated by Simon Towle of Detroit, Mich. dated 1877 on the Towles of North America. None of these sources identifies the birthplace of Philip Towle.

A search was conducted by the author for the home of Philip Towle. The name of Towle was found to definitely be English in origin. Joseph Dow's contention that he was of Irish ancestry can not be supported. The name was very common in the 16th and 17th centuries, especially in County Devonshire along the River Exe. The name was generally spelled TOWELL, but TOWLE was a common variant. The name was found in other counties such as London, Northampton, Norfolk and elsewhere, but to a much lessor extent.

Research was conducted by the author at the Devon Record Office, Castle, Exeter, England; at the West Country Studies Library, Exeter, England; at the Royal Genealogical Society Library, London; at the Public Record Office, London; at the Newberry Library, Chicago, Illinois and elsewhere including the Morman Family History Center. Regretfully Devon parish registers are incomplete and all probate records for Devon were lost in WW2. Even so, based upon surviving records for Devon it seems more than

v

likely that Philip Towle came from the parish of
Crediton, County Devon, England.

For the time period from 1577 through 1650,
the name of PHILIP TOWELL/TOWLE appears some 16
times in English records. All of these entries
occurred in Co. Devon. And with two exceptions,
all of these men named Philip Towle lived in or
near the parish of Crediton. It therefore seems
quite likely that this was the home of Philip
Towle of Hampton, N.H.

One individual named Philip Towle was found
of the correct age living at Crediton in Co.
Devonshire. Perhaps he was the immigrant, since
he is not named in later records. This Philip
was named in the 1641 Protection Record for
Devonshire at Crediton. He was born about 1616
the son of PHILIP TOWELL and his wife MARGARET
WHYTE. He can't be ruled out as the Philip Towle
of Hampton, N.H.

The earliest PHILIP TOWLE found in England
resided at the parish of Lapford, Co.
Devonshire. He married there on 19 Oct. 1577
FLORANCE DOW of the parish of Winckleigh. Philip
may have been a brother of ROGER TOWLE of nearby
Colebrooke parish. Roger Towle was the great
grandfather of Philip Towle of Crediton.

From existing parish and other public
records, the author has constructed the
following pedigree. It offers one possible
solution using all of the available information.
Hopefully additional research in the future will
confirm this solution.

William Haslet Jones

MAP OF
ENGLAND

CREDITON

LONDON

EXETER

Location of the parish of Crediton
County Devonshire, England.

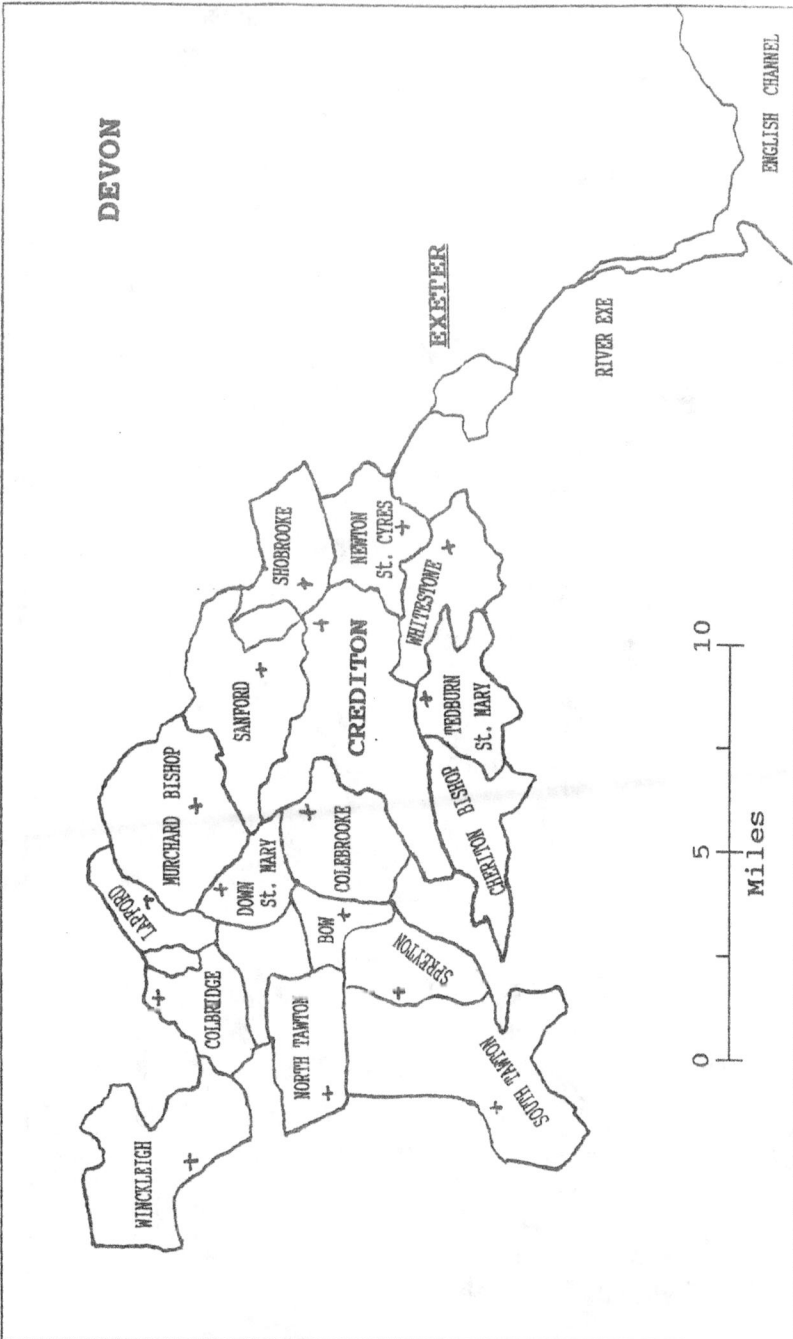

DEVON

EXETER

ENGLISH CHANNEL

RIVER EXE

SHOBROOKE

NEWTON
St. CYRES

SANDFORD

HITTISLEIGH

CREDITON

MURCHARD BISHOP

DOWN
St. MARY

TEDBURN
St. MARY

CHERITON
BISHOP

LAPFORD

COLEBROOKE

COLEBRIDGE

BOW

WINCKLEIGH

NORTH TAWTON

SPREYTON

SOUTH TAWTON

Miles

0   5   10

viii

TOWLE FAMILY Co. DEVON

1. **ROGER TOOLIE [TOWLE]** Colebrooke. He was born about 1545. He could have been the son of JOHN TOWYLL named in the 1524 Subsidy Roll for the adjoining parish of Newton St. Cyres, or the ROBERT TOLY named in the same 1524 Subsidy Roll at Down St. Mary parish. Roger used both names for his sons. On 19 May 1566 he married at Colebrooke **JOAN TAYLOR**. No burial record for either parent was found.

   Towle entries at Colebrooke end by 1589. At that time a terrible plague swept through Devonshire. It may be the reason why the Towles moved to the adjacent parish of Crediton. Based upon parish records, Roger and Joan were the parents of the following children. All baptized at Colebrooke.

   Children: 2. **JOHN**, bp 12 June 1566, md. 4 Dec. 1588 **JOAN KENTFALL**.
   3. **EDMOND**, bp 23 Nov. 1568.
   4. **ROBERT**, bp 11 Mar. 1569/70, His will dated 1620 at Sandford [Devon Record office, 136w, lost]
   5. **CHRISTOPHER**, see below.
   6. **RICHARD**, bp c1571, md. _____, had: **GEORGE** bp 19 Feb. 1588/9.
   7. **MARGARET**, bp 30 May 1579.
   8. **THOMASINE**, bp 18 Mar. 1584.

2. **CHRISTOPHER TOWELL [TOWLE]** Crediton. He was born about 1570 probably the son of Roger Toolie of nearby Colebrooke parish. The earliest Towle names found in the parish register of Crediton begin in 1592. [note: the parish register begins in 1564] The name of the wife of Christopher is unknown. No burial record for either parent was

found. Christopher, based upon parish records, was the father of the following children all baptized at Crediton.

Children: 9. PHILIP, see below.
10. GEORGE, bp 5 July 1592, md. MARGARET _____, She buried 11 Sep. 1641. Had: RICHARD, bp 7 Sep. 1625; DOROTHIE, bp 6 Jan. 1627/8.
11. JOHN, bp 26 Apr. 1593, bur. 24 Jan. 1626/7, md. MARGARET _____, She bur. 20 Aug. 1643. Had: PETER, bp 5 July 1611; JOAN, bp 13 Apr. 1622.
12. NATHANIAL, bp 14 July 1595, bur. 10 July 1649. Named in 1641 Devon Protection Record. m.1, 8 May 1625 ELIZABETH TUCKER, dau. of WILLIAM TUCKER. She bp 30 Oct. 1607 at Lapford., bur. 17 Oct. 1631; m.2, ELIZABETH TREMBLETT, dau. of WILLIAM TREMBELL, she bp 21 Nov. 1616 at Whitestone. Had: by 2nd wife: SUSANNAH, bp 15 Sep. 1633.
13. WILLIAM, bp c1600, md. BRIDGET _____, Had: THOMAS, bp 29 Sep. 1633; JOHN, bp 21 Mar. 1640/1, d.y.; JOHN, bp 2 Apr. 1648, bur. 14 Apr. 1651.
14. CHRISTOPHER, bp 5 Oct. 1606.

9. PHILLIP TOWELL [TOWLE] Crediton. He was born about 1590 probably an unnamed son of CHRISTOPHER. Philip was buried 20 April 1631 at Crediton. He was a carpenter by trade. He married first on 9 June 1610 at Crediton MARGARET WHYTE. She was the daughter of JOHN

and JUDITH WHYTE. MARGARET was baptized 19 July 1591. She died prior to 11 June 1624 when he married second ELIZABETH BARLYSYN. She survived him and was buried 26 April 1649 as Widow ELIZABETH TULE. The will of PHILLIP TUELL of Crediton is named in the records of the Court of the Principle Register of Bishop of Exeter for 1631. Regretfully all Devon wills were destroyed in World War 2. Based on surviving records, PHILIP had the following children all baptized at Crediton. See the WHYTE FAMILY Section on page 5 or her ancestry.

Children: 15. PHILIP, b. c1616, named in 1641 Prot. Record. See below.
16. ROGER, b. c1618?. See Appendix.
17. ANNE, b. c1620, md. 21 Oct. 1642 THOMAS MORTYMER.
18. JOAN, bp 29 Feb. 1622/3, bur. 29 May 1625.

by 2nd wife:
19. ELIZABETH, bp 12 July 1626, md. 15 Oct. 1650 NICHOLAS RICHARDS.
20. MARTHA, bp 6 Feb. 1627/8, bur. 11 Sep. 1628.
21. GEORGE, bp 6 July 1629, bur. 19 Apr. 1695, Weaver, Wife ELIZABETH bur. 30 Dec. 1687.

15. PHILIP TOWLE. Crediton. He is named in the 1641 Devon Protection Record for Crediton. He was probably the son of PHILIP [9]. In those days it was quite common to name the eldest son for the father. No marriage record or burial record for this PHILIP TOWLE was found at Crediton or adjacent area. Perhaps he emigrated to Hampton, N.H. after the death of his step-mother in 1649.

PHILIP TOWLE, HAMPTON, N.H.

Some twenty years later we find a PHILLIPE TOOLE marrying ARMINELL COMMONS on 31 Aug. 1663 at Crediton. He is named in the 1674 Devon Hearth Rolls, under "the poore of Crediton." He had one chimney. While we can't rule him out that he is the same Philip Towle, I believe he was a younger man. There is also the question of whether or not TOOLE equals TOWELL/TOWLE.

PHILIP TOWLE, HAMPTON, N.H.

WHYTE FAMILY

1. **JOHIS WHYTE** . Crediton. He was born about 1530. He was buried there on 14 April 1574. His widow **JOAN WHYTE** was buried there on 12 Dec. 1582. Parish records are incmplete. No doubt there were additional children.

Children: i. **ROBERT**, bur. 28 Dec. 1561.
   (2) ii. **JOHN**, bp 23 Mar. 1561/2,
       d. 9 July 1612.
   iii. **MARGARET**, bp 1 Sep. 1568.

2. **JOHN WHYTE** [JOHIS 1] He was bp at Crediton 23 Mar. 1561/2. He was buried there on 9 July 1612. He married about 1585 **JUDITH** _____. Widow **JUDITH WHYTE** was buried there on 29 April 1638. **JOHN WHYTE** was named in the 1592 Tithe Roll for Crediton (D.R.O., A-13; Crediton) They had at least the following children born at Crediton.

Children: (3) i. **MARGARET**, bp 19 July 1591, md. 9 June 1610 **PHILIP TOWELL**.
   ii. **ELIZABETH**, bp 25 Aug. 1599.
   iii. **GEORGE**, bp 25 Aug. 1599.
   iv. **JUDITH**, bp 19 Jan. 1599/1600.
   v. **GILES**, b. c1603, md. _____. Had: **GILBTE**, bp 21 Aug. 1625; **JUDITH**, bp 16 July 1628; **DOROTHIE**, bp 28 Dec. 1591.
   vi. **JOHN**, bur. 24 Nov. 1592.

3. **MARGARET WHYTE** [JOHN 2] She was bp 19 July 1591 and married 9 June 1610 **PHILIP TOWELL**. See PHILIP TOWLE #9.

HAMPTON, N.H.

15. **PHILIP TOWLE.** Hampton, N.H. he may be the
PHILIP TOWLE found in 1641 at Crediton, Co.
Devon. He was born about 1616. Just when he
emigrated is not known with certainty. His
name is not found at Hampton in any early
land owner records. Philip was buried 20
Dec. 1696 at Hampton. His will is dated 18
Dec. 1696 and was proved 25 May 1697 at New
Castle, N.H. he was at Hampton by 19 Nov.
1657 when he married **ISABELLA AUSTIN,** the
daughter of **FRANCIS** and **ISABEL (BLAND)**
AUSTIN. She was born about 1633 at
Colchester, England and died at Hampton,
N.H. 7 Dec. 1719. She was arrested on
suspicion of witchcraft, at a trial held at
Hampton on 7 Sep. 1680 and jailed. She was
released the following year after **ISAAC**
MARSTON and **JOHN REDMAN** posted her bail.
[see Appendix]

He signed the Oath of Allegiance 25 April
1678 and was freed from training 23 June
1681.

The will of Philip Towle reads:

In the name of God Amen; I Phillip Towle of Hampton in
the Providence off Newhampshire in New England Senior,
being sick and weake off Body * * *
Impr I give and bequeath unto Esabell my well beloved
wife all my Stork of Cattoll of all soarts what soever
and all my Moveabell Goods within dors and without to be
all at her disposeing off ffor her Comfortabell
livelyhood And ffor her to dispose off among my children
according to her Discretion: I allso give unto her three
cows to be kept, and ffouer Sheep and Two Swine to be
kept and Maintained yearly and every yeare by my
Executours During her naturall life or her day off
mariage as allso twelve bushells of Indian Corne Dureing
the terme above said to be paid by my Executours.
Item I Give and bequeath unto my well beloved son
Phillip Towle all that land in his possesion where his

house Standeth; allso one Share of the Cow Com'ons in
Hampton and one Aker of meadow or Marsh att the North
East of my Meadow by the great Boars Head I Allso give
unto him my grant of land in the north Division Comonly
so called -

Item I guive and bequeath unto my well beloved Son
Joshu Towle all that land that he have in his possession
where his house standeth.

It I give and bequeath unto Benjamin Towle my well
beloved Son all that Land he have In his possession
where his house Standeth Allso one share off the Cow
Com'on off the towne off Hampton as Allso my marsh and
that ground that belong to my share off the great ox
com'on in Hampton.

Item I give unto my well beloved Sons Joseph and
Caleb Towle, my Dwelling house Baren; orchard and all my
lott where Sayd House Standeth to be Eualey devided
betaen them Joseph to have his halfe nex John Blaks lott
where sayd Josephs house stands I allso give unto them
Joseph and Caleb one Share off the Cow Com'ons in
hampton I allso give unto them my Tenn akers off Marsh
be it more or less towardes the Clam Bancje or beyond
the landing place, as allso my Share of upland on the
great ox co'mone and all my Marsh by the great Boares
head Excepting Phillips acker all to be Eaqualy Divided
betwen them; with the proviso that they performe to
theire Mother what I have ordered them as Executors in
ye Artickell of this my Will; Reserveing to my wife
Dureing her natureall Life or to hir Day of Marryage the
use off one off my flier Roomes She to have her choyce,
and to be kept in Repaire by my Executors

I Doe make Constitute and appoint my Well beloved
sons Joseph Towle and Caleb Towle, to bee my Soale
Executors to this my last Will and Testament them or
either of them If one day or Renownce his Executor Shipp
then the other to be Executout a Lone; and ffor the
performance and Declareing this to be my last Will and
Testament I the said Phillip Towle Senr have here unto
put my hand and ffixed my Seale this Eighteenth day of
December in the yeare off our Lord Sixtenn Hundred ninty
and Six in the Eight yeare off the Reigne off our
Sovereigne lord William the third by the Grace of God
king off Great Brittaine, ffrance, and Ireland Deffender
off the Faith &c:

PHILIP TOWLE, HAMPTON, N.H.

Witnesses: Phillip Towle Senr
  John Smith Senr   his X mark & Seale
  Samuell Smith
  Henry Dow

[Proved May 25, 1697] Probate Records, vol. 2, p. 27]

The inventory of the estate of Philip Towle is
dated 14 Jan. 1696/7 and was appraised by Henry
Dow and John Smith. it reads in part:

> Inv. Taken of estate of Phillip Towle, who died 20
> Dec. 1696 14 Jan. 1696/7. Amount £240..5..0 Signed
> by henry Dow, John Smith & John Dearborn.

Children: 26. PHILIP, b. 3 May 1659, d. 17
               June 1717, md 30 Sep. 1714
               Wid. MARTHA (JACKSON)
               (BOULTER) DOW. No ch.
           27. CALEB, b. 17 May 1661, slain
               by Indians 13 June 1677.
           28. JOSHUA, b. 29 June 1663, d.
               25 Sep. 1715, md 2 Dec.
               1686 SARAH REED.
           29. MARY, b. 12 Nov. 1665, d.y.
           30. JOSEPH, b. 4 May 1669 (twin)
               d. 4 Sep. 1757, m.1, 14
               Dec. 1693 MEHITABLE HOBBS,
               m.2, 27 Jan. 1707/8 MARY
               WARD, m.3, 4 Mar. 1730/1
               SARAH HOBBS.
           31. BENJAMIN, b. 4 May 1669
               (twin), d. 29 May 1759, md
               7 Nov. 1693 SARAH BORDEN.
           32. FRANCIS, b. 1 Aug. 1671, d.
               about 25 Feb. 1705/6, md.
               26 July 1698 PRUDENCE
               RUSSELL.
           33. JOHN, b. 23 July 1674, d.y.
           34. CALEB, b. 14 May 1678, d. 20
               Sep. 1763, md. 14 Apr.
               1698 ZIPPORAH BRACKETT.

PHILIP TOWLE, HAMPTON, N.H.

SECOND GENERATION

26. **PHILIP TOWLE** [PHILIP 15] He was born 3 May
1659 and died 17 June 1717. He married 30
Sep. 1714 Widow **MARTHA (JACKSON)(BOULTER)**
DOW. No children. His will was written 31
May 1709 when he entered military service.
he signed the Oath of Allegiance 25 April
1678 at Hampton. The inventory of his
estate was taken 13 July 1717 by Joseph
Smith and Joshua Wingate. It mentions a
widow. Amount £135..2..0. His will reads
as follows:

> I Phillip towl of Hampton in New Hampshr being in good
> health & Sound memory: And now going in to Her majestys
> Service & not knowing how God may deel with me Do make
> & declare this my last will & testament.
> Imprimes I Give my Sole to God hoping in his mercy in
> Jesus Christ for pardon of all my Sins; & my body to ye
> dust from whence it was taken to be buryed in Christ an
> manner - & my worldly Estate after my Just Debts are
> paid - I give and bequev unto my Brother Caleb whether
> Real or personal & appynt my above named brother Caleb
> towl my Executor to this my last will & testament in
> testimony where of I Sett my hand & Seal this 31: day of
> may 1709: in ye eighth yeare of her majestys Queen ann
> her Reign over Great Britans &c.
>
> Signed Sealed & declared   The marke & Seal of
> before us witnesses: Philip X towl [seal]
>   Robert Drake
>   Joshua Wingate
> Test Joseph Smith Justice of Pece
>   ]proved Sep. 6, 1717]

28. **JOSHUA TOWLE** [PHILIP 15] He was born 29
June 1663 at Hampton, N.H. and died 23 Sep.
1715. He married 2 Dec. 1686 **SARAH REED**.
His will was dated 2 Nov. 1714 and proved 6
Dec. 1715. Inventory taken 5 Dec. 1715,
£131..15..0.

In the name of God Amen. I Joshua Towl of hampton in the Province of new-Hampshire in New England, Husbandman, being weak in body but of perfect mind & memory and knowing that it is appointed to men once to dye Do make & ordain this my last will & Testament that is to Say * * *

And as to the Worldly Estate with which it hath pleased God to bless me, I give & dispose of the same in manner & form following. That is to say.

Imprimis I will that all my honest debts with the charges of my Burial be well & truly paid in convenient time after my Decease by my Executor hereafter named.

Item, I give & Bequeath to my well Beloved wife Sarah all my Household Goods, Cattle & Moveables to be wholy at her disposal, She paying to my Daughter Hannah Gilman as hereafter ordered. I also give to my Said wife the use & Improvement of my Dwelling House which I now live in with all my Land, messages & Tennements (Excepting six acres hereafter mentioned) during her natural life.

Item, To my Beloved son Joshua Towl I give & Bequeath four acres of upland joining upon the land of my Brother Philip Towl in Hampton together with the Dwelling House standing upon the said land. I also give to my Said Son all other my Houses, Lands, Messages, Tennements (Execpt what is hereafter mentioned) after the Decease of my wife.

Item, To my Beloved Daughter Sarah Towl I give & Bequeath two acres of Land joining upon the land of Elisha Smith in Hampton.

Item, To my Beloved Daughter Hannah Gilman (She having already received part of her Portion) I give five pounds to be paid by Sarah my wife in Cattle or good Merchantable Provision at Money Price.

And I Constitute make & Ordain my Beloved Brother Caleb Towl & my Beloved Son Joshua Towl Executors of this my will. And I do hereby utterly Revoke & Disavoll all other former Wills, legacies & Executors by me in any ways before this time named, willed & Bequeathed, Ratifying & Confirming this & no other to be my Last Will & Testament. In witness Whereof I have hereto Set my Hand & Seal this second Day of November In the year of our Lord One Thousand Seven Hundred and fourteen.

Isaac Smith
Willm Haniford
Edmund Rand

The Mark of
Joshua Towl

Children: 35. **HANNAH**, b. 23 Sep. 1690, md.
CARTEE GILMAN of Exeter,
N.H., school teacher. Son
of **DANIEL & ALICE (CARTEE)
GILMAN**. He b. c1680, d.
1753.
36. **JOSHUA**, b. c1692, d. 24 Nov.
1752, md. 6 Feb. 1713
SARAH, d/o **THOMAS BROWN**.
37. **SARAH**,

30. **JOSEPH TOWLE [PHILIP 15]** He was born 4 May
1669 a twin and died 4 Sep. 1757. He
married first 14 Dec. 1693 **MEHITABLE**, d/o
JOHN HOBBS. She born 28 Feb. 1673. He
married second 27 Jan. 1707/8 **MARY WARD**. He
married third 4 Mar. 1731 **SARAH**, d/o **MORRIS
HOBBS**. His will dated 20 Sep. 1754, was
proved 26 Oct. 1757. Called Sargent. Her
will dated 16 April 1762 was proved 26 May
1762.

In the Name of God Amen - I Joseph Towle of Hampton
in the province of New Hampshire Yeoman being Weak in
Body * * *
Item I give & Bequeath to my beloved Wife Sarah one
hundred pounds of Pork - fifty pounds of Beef - twelve
bushels of Corn one peck of Beans - one peck of potatoes
two bushels of Malt - four bushels of Apples - two
pounds of Tallow - one barrel of Syder two Fleeces of
Sheeps Wool & Keeping for One Cow Summer & Winter yearly
& Every year During her Widowhood to be found & Provided
for & unto my Said Wife by my Said Executors - also one
Room in my Dwelling house During her Widowhood - I also
give her to her Own Disposal all the Goods She Bro't me

at Marriage all which is in Lieu of her Right of Dower
or power of thirds -

Item I Give & Bequeath to my Son John Towle ten
shillings New Tenor Bills of Credit to be paid by my
Said Executors -

Item I Give & bequeath to my Son Joseph Towle twenty
pounds Old Tenor to be paid by my Said Executors -

Item I Give & Bequeath to my Son James Towle twenty
pounds Old Tenor to be paid by my Said Executors -

Item I Give & Bequeath to my Son Jonathan Towle
twenty Pounds Old Tenor to be paid by my Said Executors

Item I give & bequeath to my daughter Mary Page
twenty pounds Old Tenor to be paid by my Said Executors

Item I Give & Bequeath to my daughter Mehitable Brown
twenty pounds Old Tenor to be paid by my Said Executors

Item I Give & Devise to my Grand Son Joseph Towle son
of my Son Amos Towle Deceased my Dwelling house & Barn
& all my Land thereunto Belonging * * * And my Will is
that my aforesaid Grand Son Joseph Towle when he arrives
to twenty One Years of Age Should Convey his Interest in
the Estate of his Said Father Deceas'd to his Brother
Amos Towle then to hold my Said house & Barn * * *

Item I Give & Bequeath to my Grand Son Simon Towle
Son of My Said Son Amos Deceas'd the Sum of five hundred
Pounds in Good passable Bills of Credit of the Old Tenor
& form in Case he shall Convey his Interest in the
Estate of his Said Father to his Brothers Joseph & Amos
aforesaid when he Shall come to the Age of twenty One
years to be paid by my Said Grand Sons Joseph & Amos
when my said Grand Son Simon comes to the age aforsaid
* * *

Item I Give & Bequeath to my Grand Daughter Hannah
Towle Daughter of my Said Son Amos Dec'd five shillings
New Tenor to be paid by my Said Executors -

Lastly I do hereby Ordain & appoint my aforesaid Son
Jonathan Towle of Rye in Said Province yeoman & Joshua
Lane Cordwainer of Hampton afores'd Joint Executors of
this my last Will & Testament - And hereby I do Revoke
all other Wills by me heretofore made In Witness Whereof
I have hereunto Set my hand & Seal the twentieth Day of
Sept in the twenty eighth year of his majisty's Reign
Annoque Domini One thousand Seven hundred & fifty four -

PHILIP TOWLE, HAMPTON, N.H.

Witnesses:
John Smith
Jeremiah Towle & Daniel Philbrick

his
Joseph + Towle
mark

Inventory, attested Dec. 28, 1757; amount, £5777..7..6;
signed by Philip Towle and John Nay; addition of £25..0
made Feb. 21, 1758.

Will of Sarah Towle reads as follows:

In the Name of God Amen april ye sixteenth 1762 I Sarah
Towle of Hampton in ye Province of New Hampshire in New
England Tayleress Being weak in Body * * *
Imprimis I Give & Bequeath to my sister Mary Hobbs
all my Estate both Real & Personnally of All Sorts &
Every kind to her & her Assigns forever.
I likewise Constitute make And ordain Morris Hobbs of
Sd Hampton Sole Executor * * *

her
Sarah X Towle
mark

Witnesses: Jonathan Towle Sr, Hobbs, John Weeks

Children; 38. JOHN, b. 26 June 1694, d. 5
Dec. 1786, md. 15 Nov.
1721 LYDIA PAGE, d/o
CHRISTOPHER PAGE.
39. JOSEPH, b. 31 Mar. 1696, d.
30 June 1787, md. 11 Nov.
1724 SARAH DALTON, d/o
PHILEMON DALTON.
40. JAMES, b. 10 Dec. 1698, d.
14 Apr. 1756, md. 22 July
1725 KEZIA PERKINS, d/o
ABRAHAM PERKINS.
41. MARY, b. 11 Mar. 1701, d. 14
Nov. 1783, md. 4 Jan. 1724
JONATHAN PAGE, s/o
CHRISTOPHER PAGE. Had:
MEHITABEL, b. 15 Oct.
1724; JONATHAN, b. 7 Apr.
1727, MARY, b. 10 Jan.

1729, SIMON, b. 15 June
1731.
42. JONATHAN, b. 5 Apr. 1703, d.
23 Apr. 1791, md. 10 Feb.
1728 ANNA NORTON, d/o
BONAS NORTON. 7 children.
43. MEHITABEL, b. 14 Aug. 1706,
d. 2 Jan. 1776, md. 2 May
1729 THOMAS BROWN, s/o
BENJAMIN BROWN. 4 ch.
by 2nd wife:
44. AMOS, b. 13 Nov. 1711, d. 16
July 1754, md. HANNAH
BROWN, d/o ROBERT DRAKE.
6 children.

31. BENJAMIN TOWLE [PHILIP 15] He was born 4
May 1669 a twin and died 29 May 1759. He
married 7 Nov. 1693 SARAH BORDEN. Lived
at Hampton, N.H. She born about 1671
and died 22 June 1759, aged 88 years of
fever. His will dated 13 Feb. 1758 was
proved 1759.

In the Name of God Amen the thirteenth day of February
1758 I Benjamin Towle of Hampton in the Province of New
Hampshire in New England Husbandman being weak in Body
* * *
Imprimis I Give & Bequeath unto my Beloved Wife Sarah
Towle the Improment of the East half of my Dwelling
House And Barn dureing Life, and all my moveables in my
House And one half of my Stock of Cattle horses Sheep &
Swine forever And also one Third of my Real Estate
dureing life.
Item I Give & Bequeath to my Son Benjamin Towle the
West half of my Dwelling House And one half of my Barn
And the Other half of my Said House & Barn I give unto
my Said Son After the Deceas of my Said Wife And one
half of all my Estate in Hampton Both real & Personall
to Improve dureing Life and then to go to Rebeckah Towle
the Wife of Said Benjamin to Improve till my Grand Son
Jacob Towle Shall come to the age of Twenty one Years
And then to go to Said Jacob & to Assigns forever.

- 14 -

Item I Give & Bequeath to my Son Elisha Towle my House & Barn where he now lives & one Half of All my Estate in Hampton both Real & personall to him 7 his assigns forever.

Item I Give & Bequeath to my Grand Son John Sleeper my right of Land in Cantabury to him & to his assogns forever -

Item I Give & Bequeath to my Daughter Mary Page Thirty Pounds Old Tenor to be raised & levied out of my Estate & Paid by my Son Benjamin.

Item I Give & Bequeath to my Daughter Tabathy Tuck Thirty Pounds of Old Tenor to be raised & levied out of my Estate and paid by my Son Elisha.

Item I Give & Bequeath to my Daughter Patience Hobbs Thirty Pounds Old Tenor to be raised & levied out of my Estate And Paid by my Son Benjamin.

Item I Give & Bequeath to my Daughter Hapzabah Page Thirty pounds Old Tenor to be raised & levied out of my Estate & Paid by my Son Elisha.

Item I Give & Bequeath to my Daughter Sarah Clifford Thirty Pounds Old Tenor to be raised & levied out of my Estate & Paid by my Sons Benjamin & Elisha.

I give & Bequeath to my Sons Benjamin Towle & Elisha Towle All my Estate that is not mentioned in this Will.

I likewise constitute make & ordain my Sons Benjamin Towle & Elisha Towle and my Son in Law John Page to be my Executors * * *

Witnesses:
John Weeks
James Leavit
Sambon Chandler

his
Benjamin + Towle
mark

Inventory, attested Aug. 29, 11759, £7110..1..0 signed by Joshua Lane and James Leavitt.

Children: 45. **MARY**, b. 20 May 1695, d. 17 Dec. 1783, m.1, 18 July 1718 **JOHN SLEEPER**, m.2, 29 Mar. 1727 **THOMAS PAGE**. Had: **JOHN**.
46. **TABITHA**, b. 1 May 1697, d. 12 Aug. 1766, md. 22 Feb. 1721 **JONATHAN TUCK**. Had: **JOHN**,

b. 15 Dec. 1721; BETHIAH,
b. 17 Mar. 1723; MARY, b.
6 July 1727; JONATHAN, b.
19 May 1729; SAMUEL, b.
20 Mar. 1731; ABIGAIL, bp
23 June 1734; JONATHAN,
bp 10 Oct. 1736; TABITHA,
bp 15 Aug. 1739.

47. ABIGAIL, b. 16 Sep. 1699, d.
13 May 1716.

48. MARTHA, b. c1701, d. unmd 1
Mar. 1730.

49. PATIENCE, b. 8 June 1704, md.
17 Feb. 1725 STEPHEN HOBBS.
Settled at Kensington, N.H.
Had: NOAH, b. 30 Aug. 1726;
ABIGAIL, b. 22 Jan. 1727.

50. HEPHZIBAH, b. 20 Oct. 1706,
md. 27 Feb. 1729 JOHN PAGE.
Settled at Kensington, N.H.
8 children.

51. SARAH, b. 2 May 1709, md. 22
Jan. 1734 WILLIAM CLIFFORD.

52. BENJAMIN, b. 24 May 1711,
d.y.

53. BENJAMIN, b. 3 May 1713, d.
24 June 1768, md. 30 Jan.
1735 REBECCA GARLAND.

54. ELISHA, b. 23 July 1715, md.
5 Mar. 1738 ANN VITTUM.

34. **CALEB TOWLE** [PHILIP 15] He was born 14 May
1678 and died 20 Sep. 1763. He married 14
Apr. 1698 ZIPPORAH BRACKETT d/o Capt.
ANTHONY & SUSANNAH (DRAKE) BRACKETT. She
born 28 Sep. 1679 and died 14 Aug. 1756.
Owned a sawmill. Res. Hampton and Chester,
N.H. His will dated 12 Sep. 1763.

> In the name of God Amen this twelvth Day of September
> In the Year of our Lord, One thousand Seven Hundred &
> Sixty three and in the third Year of the Reign of King
> George the third over Great Britain &c.
>   I Caleb Towle of Hampton in the Province of New
> Hampshire Yeoman * * *

Item I Give & Devise to my Son Philip Towle one Acre of Salt marsh lying at a place called the Great-Boars-head being on the North East side of the Marsh of my brother Joseph Towle Deceased also my land where he now lives to him his heirs & Assigns.

Item I Give & Devise to my Son Caleb Towle my one Hundred Acre lott of Land in Chester in Said Province lying in the North Division Number 12 to him his Heirs & Assigns.

Item I Give & Devise to my Son Anthony Towle one half of that whole Right in Chester afores'd which was originally of Jonathan Dearborn also my Land where he now lives to him his Heirs & Assigns.

Item I Give & Devise to my Son Zachoriah my Sixty acre lott of Land in Chester afores'd lying in the fourth Division so Called to him his Heirs & Assigns.

Item I Give & Bequeath to the Heirs of my Son Matthias Towle Twenty pounds old tenor to be paid by my Executors.

Item I give & Devise to my Son jeremiah Towle all my land where he now lives also two acres of Swamp Land lying on the Southerly Side of the Road before his now Dwelling house also one half of that peice of Salt marsh in Hampton afores'd which I purchased of Sam'l Marston Deceas'd to him his heirs & Assigns.

Item I give 7 Devise to my Son Francis Towle my Eighty Acre lott of Land in Chester afores'd also my whole Right in Said Chester Excepting what is herein Dispos'd off also one half of my interest in the Saw Mill afores'd also my two Twenty acre Lotts of Land where he now lives to him his Heirs & Assigns.

Item i give & Devise to my Son Nathaniel Towle my Dwelling house meaning that my Daughter Hanah Should live therein as herein after mentioned also all my Homested Excepting what is herein after Devised to my Said Daughter hanah & to my Grandson Samuel Towle Son of the aforesaid Matthias I also give & Devise to my Son Nathaniel my peice of Salt marsh in Hampton at a place called the Clam banks also one half of that peice of wood land in Hampton afores'd at a place Called Morsey Swamp also one half of that three Quarters of a Share of Land at Rocky Nook so called also my peice of Salt Marsh at the Boarshead aforesaid also my meddow ground at a

- 17 -

PHILIP TOWLE, HAMPTON, N.H.

place Called deep Run in Hampton afores'd to him his
Heirs & Assigns.

Item I give & Bequeath to Each of the Children of my
Daughter Elizabeth Brown Deceas'd five Shillings new
tenor Bills of Credit to be paid by my Said Executors.

Item I give & Bequeath to my Daughter Hanah Towle the
free use & Improvement of the Easterly End of my
Dwelling House also the Improvement of one half of my
orchard also the Improvement of one acre of Land Joyning
to the East End of my House so Running Easterly on the
Road Dureing the End of my House so Running Easterly on
the Road Dureing the time of her being unmarried then to
Return to my Sd Son Nathaniel I also Give to my Sd
Daughter Hannah Twelve Bushells of Indian Corn two
Bushells of malt one Hundred weight of poark one Hundred
weight of Beef Paustering & hay Sufficent for keeping
two Cows & four Sheep Dureing the time of her being
unmarried and it is my will that the same should be
found & provided for my said Daughter by my said Son
Nathaniel yearly & every year During the time aforesaid
and in Case She should see fitt to marry then it is my
will that she should have two Hundred pounds old tenor
to be paid by my aforesaid Sons Jeremiah & Nathaniel I
also give to my Said Daughter to her own Disposal all my
Household Goods Stock of Cattle & Sheep.

Item I give & devise to my aforesaid Grandson Samuel
Towle Twenty five acres of Land of off the Easterly End
of the land where my Dwelling House now Stands also one
half of my peice of wood Land in Hampton at a place
Called morsey Swamp also one half of that peice of marsh
I purchased of Sam'l Marston Deceas'd also one half of
that three quarters of a share of Land at Rocky nook so
Called also one half of my new Barn to him his Heirs &
Assigns.

Lastly I do by these presents Constitute & appoint my
two sons Philip & Jeremiah to be Executors * * *

Witnesses: Caleb X Towle
  Josiah Dearborn   Mark
  Joshua James & Christo'r Toppan

Children: 55. PHILIP, b. 18 Aug. 1698, d.
             15 Feb. 1785, md. 4 Mar.
             1724 LYDIA DOW.

- 18 -

56. ELIZABETH, b. 2 Dec. 1699,
    d. 13 Mar. 1741, m.1,
    JOHN FELLOWS, m.2, 1 Jan.
    1724 JOSIAH BROWN
57. CALEB, b. 9 May 1701, d. 3
    Feb. 1795, md. 18 Jan.
    1727 REBECCA PRESCOTT.
58. ANTHONY, b. 30 Apr. 1703,
    md. 7 Nov. 1734 SARAH
    HOBBS.
59. ZACHARIAH, b. 13 Aug. 1705,
    d. 5 Aug. 1787, md. 15
    May 1728 ANNE GODFREY.
60. MATTHIAS, b. 13 Aug. 1707,
    d. before 16 Sep. 1787,
    md. 13 Dec. 1733 HANNAH
    JENNESS or HANNAH HOIT.
61. JEREMIAH, b. 12 Dec. 1709,
    d. 7 Nov. 1800, m.1, 23
    Jan. 1740 HANNAH
    DEARBORN, m.2, 18 Aug.
    1791 widow SARAH
    (SANBORN) TUCK. No ch.
62. FRANCIS, b. 13 Jan. 1711/2,
    d. 11 Nov. 1804, m.1,
    PRUDENCE _____, m.2,
    4 June 1738 JUDITH
    SARGENT.
63. HANNAH, b. 28 Mar. 1714, d.
    28 Aug. 1789.
64. NATHANIEL, b. 25 May 1716,
    d. 9 Apr. 1803, md. 17
    Sep. 1740 LYDIA TILTON.
65. ABRAHAM, b. 29 Nov. 1719,
    d.y.
66. SAMUEL, b. 9 Sep. 1722, d.
    14 May 1736.

THIRD GENERATION

36. JOSHUA TOWLE [JOSHUA 28] He was born about
    1692 at Hampton and died 24 Nov. 1752. He
    married 6 Feb. 1713 SARAH BROWN daughter

of **THOMAS BROWN.** Administration of his estate granted 27 Dec. 1752 to son Joshua Towle.

[Bond of Joshua Towle, with Ebenezer Brown and Jonathan Dearborn, yeoman, as surities, all of Hampton, in the sum of £1000 Dec. 27, 1752; witnesses, Philip Towle and William Parker Jr.]

[Inventory, Jan. 5, 1753; amount £672..0..0; signed by John Sherburne and John Weeks.]

Children: 67. **ELIZABETH,** bp 5 Sep. 1714.
68. **JOSHUA,** b. 19 May 1716, d. 30 Aug. 1716
69. **HANNAH,** bp 2 Feb. 1718, d.y.
70. **JOSHUA,** b. 6 Dec. 1719, md. 1 Jan. 1746 **ELIZABETH SANBORN.**
71. **JOSIAH,** b. 13 Feb. 1721, twin.
72. **ABIGAIL,** b. 13 Feb. 1721, twin.
73. **EBENEZER,** b. 17 May 1724, d. 1757, md. 10 Apr. 1749 **ALICE FIFIELD.**
74. **HANNAH,** b. 12 July 1727, d. 4 Aug. 1746 unmd.
75. **SARAH,** bp 18 June 1732, d. 6 Apr. 1736.

38. **JOHN TOWLE [JOSEPH 30]** He was born 26 June 1694 and died 5 Dec. 1786. He married 15 Nov. 1721 **LYDIA PAGE,** daughter of **CHRISTOPHER PAGE.** She was born 3 Aug. 1698 and died 22 May 1772.

Children: 76. **JOHN,** b. 23 May 1723, md. 10 Jan. 1745 **MARY PAGE.**
77. **ABIGAIL,** b. Apr. 1725, m.1, 29 Nov. 1744 **SAMUEL FOGG,** m.2, **SAMUEL ROBY.**
78. **ELIPHALET,** b. 4 Sep. 1728.

79. MEHETABEL, b. 1 Apr. 1732,
    d. unmd 11 June 1822.
80. LEMUEL, b. 26 July 1737, d.
    25 Apr. 1778, md. MARY
    SHAW.

39. JOSEPH TOWLE [JOSEPH 30] He was born 31
    Mar. 1696 at Hampton and died 30 June
    1787. He married 11 Nov. 1724 SARAH
    DALTON, daughter of Dea. PHILEMON DALTON.
    She was born 19 Aug. 1704 at Hampton.

    Children: 81. JONATHAN, b. 9 Apr. 1726,
                   went to N.Y.
               82. DOROTHY, b. 15 Nov. 1728,
                   md. DANIEL PICKING of
                   Portsmouth. Had: DANIEL;
                   SARAH and THOMAS G.
               83. JOSEPH, b. 28 Dec. 1730, d.
                   28 Jan. 1820, m.1,
                   ELIZABETH TOWLE, m.2, MARY
                   (LOCKE) REDMAN.
               84. SARAH, b. 10 Sep. 1733, md.
                   11 Apr. 1754 Dr. JOSEPH
                   SANBORN of Kensington.
               85. ABIGAIL, b. 5 Nov. 1735.
               86. MARY, b. 26 Dec. 1737, d. 31
                   July 1754.
               87. AMOS, b. 3 June 1740, d. 8
                   Apr. 1812, md. 30 June
                   1763 SARAH NUDD.
               88. DANIEL, b. 7 Sep. 1743, d.
                   28 July 1754.
               89. JETHRO, b. 26 Mar. 1747, d.
                   1 Aug. 1754.

40. JAMES TOWLE [JOSEPH 30] He was born 10
    Dec. 1698 at Hampton and died 14 Apr. 1756.
    He married 22 July 1725 KEZIA PERKINS,
    daughter of ABRAHAM PERKINS. She born 25
    Apr. 1709 and died 12 Dec. 1794 at Hampton,
    by a fall in the fire. His will is dated 8
    April 1756 and was proved 9 July 1756.

PHILIP TOWLE, HAMPTON, N.H.

In the Name of God Amen the Eighth Day of April 1756
We James Towle of Hampton in the Province of New
Hampshire in New England Husbandman And Kezia Towle Wife
of Said James Towle of Hampton in Said Province Spinster
We being Weak in Body * * *

Imprimis We give & Bequeath to our Well Beloved Son
Abraham Perkins Towle the one half of All our Land &
Marsh Excepting A Peice of Land Lying Jouning to the
Land of Richard Sandborn & the Land of Lieut. Jonath'n
Levit and A Peice of Marsh in ye Spring marsh beyond the
great Crick About Two acrs more or Less And a peace of
Swomp Lying by Land of Tomas Nudd & Land of my Father
joseph Towle which Peice Contanes Five Acers at the
South End of my Lot in Said Swomp which Peices are for
our Son Jonathan Also we give to our Sd Son Abraham the
one half of all our Real Estate to him And to his
Assigns for ever And Also the one half of All our
Personall Estate.

Item we give & Bequeath to our well beloved Son James
Towle the half of all our Land & Marsh Excepting a Tract
of Land Lying between Land of Richard Sandborn & Land of
Jonathan Lovit And a Tract of Marsh in the Spring marsh
Two Acers More or Less South of the Great Crick And A
Tract of Meddow Lying Between meddow of our Father
Joseph Towle & Meddow of Thomas Nudd for my son Jonathan
And Also we give to our Said Son James the one half of
all our Real Estate to him & his Assigns forever And
Also one Half of All our Personell Estate my Two Said
Sons Abraham Perkins Towle & James Towle Equally to
devide Sd Estate At the time my Said Son James shall
Come to the Age of Twenty one years.

Item We Give & Bequeath to our Wel beloved Son
Jonathan Towle A Tract of Land Lying by the Country Road
between the Land of Richard Sandborn & Land of Jonathan
Lovit And Also A peice of Marsh Lying the South Side of
the great Crick About Two Acers And Also A Tract of
Meddow Containing Five Acers At the South end of My
Meddow And lying Between meddow of our Father Joseph
Towle And Meddow of Thomas Nudd To him & his Assigns.

Item We Give & Bequeath to our Welbeloved Daughter
Mary Silver the Sum of Twenty Pounds Old Tenor to be
leavied & Raised out of Our Estate & Paid by our Son
James Towle.

Item We Give & Bequeath to Our Welbeloved Daughter
Mehetable Perkins the Sum of Ten Pounds Old Tenor to be
Raised & Leavied out of Our Estate & Paid by our Son
Abraham Perkins Towle.

Item We Give & Bequeath to Our Welbeloved Daughter
Anna Sandborn the Sum of Ten Pounds Old Tenor to be
Raised & Levied out of Our Estate & Paid by our Son
Abraham Perkins Towle.

Item We Give & Bequeath to our Welbeloved Daughter
Huldah Towle the Sum of Ten Pounds Old Tenor to be
Raised & Leavied out of Our Estate & Paid by our Sons
Abraham Perkins Towle & James Towle.

We Likewise Constitute make & ordain our Two Sons
Abraham Perkins Towle & James Towle Executors * * *

	his
Witnesses	James + Towle
John Weeks	mark
Benjamin Mason	Kezia Towle
Joseph Towle	
Edmund Mason	

Children: 90. **MARY**, b. 3 Mar. 1728, md.
_____ **SILVER**.
91. **MEHETABEL**, bp 12 Apr. 1730,
md. 7 Apr. 1752 **ABRAHAM
PERKINS**. Lived at Rye.
Had: **ABRAHAM**.
92. **ANNA**, bp 4 Mar. 1733, d. 18
Oct. 1823, md. 12 Feb.
1755 **BENJAMIN SANBORN** of
Hampton Falls.
93. **HULDAH**, bp 14 Dec. 1735, md.
17 Aug. 1756 **MERRIFIELD
BERRY** of Rye. Had: **JAMES
T**, b. 15 Mar. 1758;
HULDAH, b. 26 Oct. 1760;
OLLY, b. 19 Sep. 1763;
EBENEZER, b. 15 Mar. 1766;
ABIGAIL, b. 26 Dec. 1768.

94. ABRAHAM PERKINS, b. 23 Apr.
1740, d. 8 Dec. 1804, md.
23 Dec. 1763 ABIGAIL
MOULTON.
95. JAMES, b. 10 May 1743, d. 14
May 1783, md. ANNA _____.
96. JONATHAN, b. 23 Aug. 1747,
md. 21 Jan. 1773 MIRIAM
MARSTON.

42. JONATHAN TOWLE [JOSEPH 30] He was born 5
April 1703 at Hampton and died 23 April
1791. He married 10 Feb. 1728 ANNA NORTON,
daughter of BONAS and LUCY (DOWNING)
NORTON. She born 20 March 1707. Res. Rye.

Children: 97. JONATHAN, b. 4 July 1729, d.
at Epsom, md. ELIZABETH
JENNESS.
98. LEVI, b. 22 Sep. 1731, md.
11 Oct. 1753 RUTH MARDEN.
99. JOSEPH, b. 21 Mar. 1733, md.
SARAH WALLIS.
100. SAMUEL, b. 5 Nov. 1735, m.1,
21 Aug. 1760 RACHEL
ELKINS, m.2, 18 Nov. 1762
ESTHER JOHNSON.
101. JAMES, b. 28 Oct. 1737.
102. ANNA, b. 28 Mar. 1741, md. 2
Dec. 1760 JOSEPH
PHILBRICK.
103. NATHAN, b. 29 May 1745.

44. AMOS TOWLE [JOSEPH 30] He was born 13 Nov.
1711 at Hampton and died 6 July 1754. He
married HANNAH DRAKE daughter of ROBERT
DRAKE. She married second 26 April 1759
JONATHAN MARSTON by whom she had four
children. Inventory of his Estate attested
30 Oct. 1754. Amount £4204..8..0; signed by
Joshua Lane and Jeremiah Towle.

Guardianship of Joseph Towle, Amos Towle, and Hannah
Towle aged less then 14 years, children of Amos Towle,
granted to Philip Towle of Hampton, yeoman, Feb. 22,
1759.

Children: 104. SARAH, b. 13 July 1742, d.
                 29 Mar. 1754.
            105. ROBERT, b. 12 Aug. 1744, d.
                 15 July 1754.
            106. JOSEPH, b. 7 Feb. 1747, d. 1
                 Apr. 1820, md. 1769
                 ELIZABETH COFFIN.
            107. AMOS, b. 6 May 1749, d. 29
                 Aug. 1825, md. ABIGAIL
                 DOW.
            108. SIMON, b. 8 Aug. 1751, d.
                 unmd.
            109. HANNAH, bp 23 Dec. 1753, md.
                 JEREMIAH MARSTON.

53. BENJAMIN TOWLE [BENJAMIN 31] He was born 3
    May 1713 at Hampton and died 24 June 1768.
    He married 30 Jan. 1735 REBECCA GARLAND,
    daughter of JACOB GARLAND.

Children: 110. HANNAH, b. 24 July 1735, md.
                 18 Nov. 1756 JEREMIAH
                 NORRIS of Epping. Had:
                 BENJAMIN bp 4 Dec. 1757.
            111. SARAH, b. 14 Apr. 1737, md.
                 11 Apr. 1755 JOSEPH
                 SANBORN.
            112. ABIGAIL, b. 24 Aug. 1739,
                 d. 22 Feb. 1756.
            113. PATIENCE, b. 16 Dec. 1741,
                 d. 15 Apr. 1765, md. 27
                 June 1763 THOMAS DRAKE.
            114. JACOB, b. 16 June 1744, md.
                 _____ MOULTON.
            115. EBENEZER, bp 5 Apr. 1747,
                 d. Oct. 1753.
            116. BENJAMIN, bp 24 Sep. 1749,
                 d. 16 Nov. 1753.

54. **ELISHA TOWLE** [**BENJAMIN** 31] He was born 23 July 1715 at Hampton. He married 5 Mar. 1738 **ANNE VITTUM**, daughter of **WILLIAM** and **ABIGAIL VITTUM**. She born 30 Nov. 1718.

Children: 117. **ELISHA**, bp 23 Sep. 1739, d. 8 Jan. 1820, md. **ANNA SANBORN**.
118. **ABIGAIL**, bp 1 Mar. 1741, d. unmd. 23 Sep. 1815.
119. **ANNE**, bp 6 Feb. 1743, d. unmd. 3 Mar. 1821.
120. **BENJAMIN**, bp 8 Dec. 1745, md. **ABIGAIL EDGERLY**, d/o **JOSEPH EDGERLY**.
121. **SARAH**, bp 25 Oct. 1747, d. 3 June 1754.
122. **MARY**, bp 15 Oct. 1749, d. 5 June 1754.
123. **JEREMIAH**, bp 10 May 1752, d. 7 June 1754.
124. **JEREMIAH**, bp 30 June 1754.
125. **SARAH**, bp 6 June 1756, d. 24 Apr. 1759.
126. **JOSHUA**, bp 14 Mar. 1758, d. 15 Mar. 1758.
127. **WILLIAM**, bp 7 June 1761.

55. **PHILIP TOWLE** [**CALEB** 34] He was born 18 Aug. 1698 and died 15 Feb. 1785. He married 4 Mar. 1724 **LYDIA DOW**, daughter of **JAMES & ESTHER DOW**. She born 5 Nov. 1700 and died 16 Apr. 1766.

Children: 128. **JABEZ**, b. 24 Nov. 1724, d. unmd. 25 Dec. 1745 at Louisburg, Canada.
129. **PHILIP**, b. 30 Mar. 1727, d. 11 June 1736.
130. **JEREMIAH**, b. 17 Aug. 1729.
131. **EZEKIEL**, b. 16 Jan. 1731, d. 13 June 1736.

PHILIP TOWLE, HAMPTON, N.H.

132. **ESTHER**, b. 16 Jan. 1734, d.
17 June 1736, md.
BENJAMIN LEAVITT.
133. **BENJAMIN**, b. 5 Jan. 1735,
d. 8 June 1736.
134. **PHILIP**, b. 20 Oct. 1737, d.
15 Mar. 1798, md. 15 Dec.
1763 **ANNE PAGE**.
135. **PATIENCE**, b. 14 Oct. 1740,
d. 29 July 1788 unmd.

57. **CALEB TOWLE [CALEB 34]** He was born 9 May
1701 and died 3 Feb. 1795 at Hawke, N.H.
He married 18 Jan. 1727 **REBECCA PRESCOTT**
daughter of **JAMES & MARIA (MARSTON)**
PRESCOTT. She born 27 Sep. 1711 and died
1795. Res. at Danville and Chester, N.H.

Children: 136. **ANNA**, b. 28 May 1728, md.
12 Mar. 1752 **EBENEZER LONG**.
137. **ELISHA**, b. 12 Jan. 1730,
md. 27 Dec. 1753
ELIZABETH BROWN.
138. **MARY**, b. 4 Nov. 1732, md. 2
Aug. 1759 **AARON QUIMBY**.
139. **JAMES**, bp 11 July 1736, d.y
140. **CALEB**, bp 11 Dec. 1737, d.
9 Aug. 1765, md. 13 Dec.
1737 **RUTH PAGE**.
141. **DANIEL**, b. 12 Oct. 1740.
142. **JEREMIAH**, b. 19 June 1745,
m.1, **19 Sep. 1765 MARY**
SARGENT, m.2, 4 Oct. 1814
HANNAH YOUNG.
143. **JAMES**, b. 31 Dec. 1747, d.
31 Dec. 1825, 13 Sep.
1768 **ABIGAIL COLBY**.
144. **MARIAH**, bp. 25 Apr. 1751,
twin.
145. **ZIPPORAH**, bp. 25 Apr. 1751,
twin.

58. **ANTHONY TOWLE [CALEB 34]** He was born 30
April 1703 and died before 1765. He
married 7 Nov. 1734 **SARAH HOBBS** daughter

of **MAURICE HOBBS**. She born 31 Oct. 1703.
Res. at Chester where he was Constable
in 1734.

Children: 146. **REUBEN**, b. 20 Nov. 1735.
147. **SAMUEL**, b. 20 Nov. 1737, d.
1793, md. 13 Mar. 1760
MARY DEARBORN.
148. **JONATHAN**, b. 10 Nov. 1739,
d. after 1777, md. **ANNA
ROBIE**, d/o **JOHN ROBIE**.
149. **PHINEAS**, b. 5 Apr. 1742.
150. **MAURICE/MORRIS**, b. 15 Feb.
1743.
151. **BRACKETT**, b. 25 Feb. 1746,
md. **NELLIE RICHARDSON**.
Rev. Service. Moved to
Vermont.
152. **SARAH**, b. 9 Jan. 1748.
153. **SIMON**, b. 19 Sep. 1749.
154. **MARY**, b. 23 Nov. 1750.
155. **ANTHONY**, b. 4 Nov. 1752, d.
1808.

59. **ZACHARIAH TOWLE [CALEB 34]** He was born 13
Aug. 1705 and died 5 Aug. 1787. He married
15 May 1728 **ANNE GODFREY** daughter of
WILLIAM GODFREY. Res. North Hampton.

Children: 156. **ABRAHAM**, b. 19 June 1728,
d.y.
157. **JANE/JEAN**, b. 4 May 1730.
158. **ABRAHAM**, b. 19 July 1732,
d. 4 Nov. 1760.
159. **ISAAC**, b. 23 Feb. 1735, d.
24 Aug. 1791, md. 14 Feb.
1754 **ELIZABETH PHILBRICK**.
She m.2, 9 Jan. 1797
JONATHAN SWAIN Esq.
160. **ZACHARIAH**, b. 8 June 1736,
d. 28 May 1741.
161. **SIMON**, b. 11 May 1740, 20
Sep. 1741.
162. **MARY/MARAH**, b. 21 July
1746, d. 9 May 1830 unmd.

PHILIP TOWLE, HAMPTON, N.H.

    163. ZACHARIAH, b. 9 Dec. 1746,
          d. 28 May 1803, md. 25
          Feb. 1768 MARY DEARBORN.

60. MATTHIAS TOWLE [CALEB 34] He was born 13
    Aug, 1707 at Hampton and died in 1768.
    Res. at Chester and Raymond, N.H. He
    married HANNAH HOIT. One source says he
    married 13 Dec. 1733 HANNAH JENNESS. The
    Admin. on his estate was granted to
    Abner Cough 9 Nov. 1763. [v.23, p. 120]

Children: 164. MATTHIAS,
         165. SAMUEL, b. c1738, d. 25 Apr.
            1796, md. RACHEL
            ELKINS.
         166. WILLIAM, b. 1740, md. c1765
            ELIZABETH PRESCOTT.
         167. HANNAH, bp 23 Sep. 1753,
            md. JOSIAH TOWLE [#176].
         168. ZIPPORAH, bp Sep. 1764.

NOTE: A MATTHIAS TOWLE of Epping left a will
    dated 22 June 1767 and was proved 25
    May 1768. It names a wife and different
    children then found in Dow and Lindsey.
    Who is right? The will reads as follows:

In the Name of God Amen the twenty second Day of June
Anno Domini 1767. I Matthias towl of Eppin in ye
Province of New Hampshire Husbandman being week in Body
* * *
Imprimis I give and Bequeath to my well beloved wife
Hannah towl one third Part of all my Real Estate for and
During her Natureal Life. Itm: I give and bequeath to my
two Sons Soloman towl and Jennes towl and to their heirs
and assigns for ever all my Real Estate and to be
equally Devided between them according to Quantity and
Quality. Itm: I give and bequeath to my Daughter moley
towl five pounds Lawful money and a Cow and to be Paid
by my Son Soloman towl as Soon as he Shall arrive to the
age of twenty one years. Itm: I give and bequeath to my
Daughter Hannah towl five pounds Lawful money and a Cow
and to be paid by my Son James towl as Soon as he Shall
arive to the age of twenty one years.

PHILIP TOWLE, HAMPTON, N.H.

and as my Personal Estate is not above mentioned, it is my will that all my Personal Estate execpt my house hold goods Shall be Sold by my Executerix to Pay the Debts as far as they will Answre.

Itm: I Likewise give to my well beloved wife all my house hold goods for the use and Benefit of her self and my Children:

I do Constetute and appoint my well beloved wife Hannah towl to be my Executerix * * *

Witnesses:
  Joseph Prescott
  Elias Philbrick
  Abraham Parker

His
Matthias X Towl
Mark

62. **FRANCIS TOWLE [CALEB 43]** He was born 13 Jan. 1711 and died March 1790. He married first **PRUDENCE** _____. He married second 4 June 1738 **JUDITH SARGENT**, daughter of **Ensign JACOB & JUDITH (HARVEY) SARGENT**. She born 27 March 1716.

Children: 169. **FRANCIS**, md. Miss **NICHOLS** of Derry.
    170. **ZIPPORAH**, b. 26 May 1744, d. 11 Nov. 1804, md. Capt. **JOHN DEARBORN**. He b. 1746, d. 1794. Had: **JOHN**, b. 3 Aug. 1763; **DOROTHY**, b. 12 July 1765; **JEREMIAH**, b. 8 Jan. 1768; **LEVI**, b. 25 Dec. 1769; **FRANCIS**, b. 3 Apr. 1772; **JACOB**, b. 8 May 1774; **ELIZABETH**, b. 12 Sep. 1776; **ZIPPORAH**, b. 15 June 1778; **ANNA/NANCY**, b. 12 Jan. 1781; **JOSIAH**, b. 12 Nov. 1783; **THOMAS**, b. 25 Aug. 1786; **JONATHAN**, b. 22 Aug. 1788.
    171. **JACOB**, b. c1743.

- 30 -

172. ELIZABETH, b. 2 June
     1738, md. JOSEPH TOWLE.
     [#83]
173. MARY, b. 6 May 1742, md.
     _____NORRIS.
174. HANNAH, b. 1 Mar. 1739, md.
     _____ RICHARDSON.
175. JEREMIAH, b. c1747, d. 7
     Nov. 1800, m.1, 10 June
     1781 ABIGAIL TRUE,
     m.2 SUSANNA WILSON.

64. NATHANIEL TOWLE [CALEB 34] He was born 25
May 1716. He married 17 Sep. 1740 LYDIA
TILTON. She died Oct. 1800 aged 82 years.

Children: 176. ELIZABETH, bp 29 Nov. 1741,
              d. 19 Apr. 1785.
          177. JOSEPH, bp 16 Jan. 1743, d.
              20 July 1743.
          178. HULDAH, b. 13 May 1744, d.
              3 Aug. 1746.
          179. JOSIAH, bp 11 Aug. 1745, d.
              21 July 1817, md. 10 Nov.
              1773 HANNAH TOWLE [#163].
          180. JABEZ, bp 5 Apr. 1747, d.
              20 June 1837, md. 6 Jan.
              1778 SARAH GARLAND.
          181. DANIEL, bp 11 June 1749, d.
              22 July 1754.
          182. HULDAH, bp 9 June 1751, d.
              19 July 1754.
          183. ZIPPORAH, bp 27 May 1753,
              d. 16 July 1828, md.
              ROBERT DRAKE. Had:
              DOROTHY; ABRAHAM;
              ELIZABETH; SARAH;
              NATHANIEL; DANIEL.
          184. LYDIA, bp 8 June 1755, d.
              15 Aug. 1829, md. Lt.
              JOHN LOVERING.

FOURTH GENERATION

70. JOSHUA TOWLE [JOSHUA 36] He was born 6
Dec. 1719. He married 1 Jan. 1746
ELIZABETH SANBORN, daughter of SHUBAEL
SANBORN. She born 27 Dec. 1724 and died
10 Sep. 1809.

>Children: 185. JOSHUA, b. c1752, d. 13
>Sep. 1797, md. 31 Oct.
>1771 JANE DRAKE.

73. EBENEZER TOWLE [JOSHUA 36] He was born 17
May 1724 and died in 1757. He married 10
April 1749 ALICE FIFIELD. Estate dated 28
Dec. 1757. Inventory dated 5 Feb. 1758.
Amount was £2050..19..00. Widow Alice and
two children under age 7 years mentioned.

>Children: 186. WILLIAM, b. 23 Jan. 1750,
>md. MIRIAM BURLEY.
>187. JOSHUA, b. 20 July 1753.
>188. EBENEZER, b. 21 Mar. 1756,
>md. MOLLY WELLS.
>189. PAUL, b. 21 Mar. 1756.

76. JOHN TOWLE [JOHN 38] He was born 23 May
1723. He married 10 Jan. 1745 MARY PAGE
daughter of STEPHEN PAGE.

>Children: 190. SIMON, b. 1745.
>191. JOHN, b. 1748.

80. LEMUEL TOWLE [JOHN 38] He was born 26 July
1737 and died 25 Apr. 1778. He married MARY
SHAW, daughter of GIDEON SHAW. She born 26
July 1739. She m.2, JEREMIAH PRESCOTT of
Epping.

>Children: 192. LYDIA, b. 19 Dec. 1757, md.
>17 Jan. 1781 SAMUEL HOBBS
>s/o JOSEPH HOBBS.
>193. ELIPHALET, b. 6 Oct. 1760.

194. LEMUEL, bp 12 June 1768, d.
5 Aug. 1807, md. ABIGAIL
LANE.

83. JOSEPH TOWLE [JOSEPH 39] He was born 28
Dec. 1730 and died 28 Jan. 1820. He
married first ELIZABETH TOWLE [#169].
She died Nov. 1795. He married second
MARY (LOCKE) RODMAN, daughter of SAMUEL
LOCKE. She born 14 Dec. 1746 and died
10 Aug. 1800.

Children: 195. JOSEPH, b. 1768, d. 11 Oct.
1828, md. SARAH MARSTON.

87. AMOS TOWLE [JOSEPH 39] He was born 3 June
1740 and died 8 Apr. 1812. He married 30
June 1763 SARAH NUDD, daughter of THOMAS
NUDD. She born 10 Jan. 1741 and died 12
Nov. 1820. Res. Hampton.

Children: 196. BETTY, b. 15 July 1764, d.
6 Aug. 1776.
197. DANIEL, b. 29 Oct. 1767, d.
11 June 1812, md. 13 Apr.
1793 LYDIA TOWLE [#284].
198. SALLY, bp 24 Apr. 1774, d.
27 Apr. 1843, md. JOHN
REDMAN.
199. BETTEY, b. 5 Aug. 1783, d.
5 Aug. 1860, md. JOHN
TUCK.

94. ABRAHAM PERKINS TOWLE [JAMES 40] He was
born 23 Apr. 1740 and died 8 Dec. 1804.
He married 23 Dec. 1763 ABIGAIL MOULTON
daughter of JOHN MOULTON. She born 28
Nov. 1745 and died 7 June 1825.

Children: 200. HANNAH, b. 7 Oct. 1764, d.
unmd. 13 July 1849.
201. ANNA, bp 24 Apr. 1768, md.
31 May 1789 Dea. DAVID
LOCKE of Rye & Epsom.

202. **MOLLY**, bp 3 May 1772, md. 28 Aug. 1797 **JOHN CATE** of Epsom.
203. **ABIGAIL**, bp 10 July 1774, d. 20 Nov. 1826, md. **JESSE PRESCOTT**.
204. **JAMES**, b. 26 Nov. 1776, d. 15 June 1859, md. **ABIGAIL BROWN**.

95. **JAMES TOWLE** [JAMES 40] He was born 10 May 1743 and died 14 May 1783. He married **ANN** _____. Res. at Hampton and Pittsfield.

Children: 205. **JAMES**, bp 3 May 1766, d. 16 June 1828, md. **ANNA LANE**.
206. **JONATHAN**, bp 3 Apr. 1769.
207. **DAVID**, b. 15 July 1771, d. 1 May 1828, md. **ZIPPORAH DEARBORN**.
208. **PERKINS**, bp 18 July 1773.
209. **WILLIAM**, bp 13 July 1777, d. 30 Apr. 1778.
210. **SIMON**, bp 14 July 1779, md. **MARY SANBORN**, d/o **JOHN SANBORN**. Settled in Gilmanton.

96. **JONATHAN TOWLE** [JAMES 40] He was born 23 Aug. 1747. He married 21 Jan. 1773 **MIRIAM MARSTON** of North Hampton. Removed to Chichester 1781, afterwards to Pittsfield.

Children: 211. **MOLLY**, bp 16 Oct. 1774.
212. **HULDAH**, bp 18 June 1775.
213. **JONATHAN**, bp 8 June 1777, md. **POLLY** _____.
214. **DANIEL**, bp 21 Feb. 1779.
215. **JAMES**, bp 3 June 1781.
216. **SALLY**, b. c1784.
217. **ABRAHAM PERKINS**, bp 12 Oct. 1788.

97. **JONATHAN TOWLE** [JONATHAN 42] He was born 4
July 1729 and died at Epsom, N.H. He
married **ELIZABETH JENNESS**, daughter of **JOHN
& ANNE (FOULSHAM) JENNESS**. She born 4 April
1734 at Rye. Res. at Rye.

Children: 218. **SIMON**, b. 1753, md.
ELIZABETH MARDEN.
219. **MARY**, b. 1755, md. 6 Jan.
1774 **JAMES HOBBS.**
220. **LEVI**, b. 1757, m.1, **MARY
LOCKE**, m.2, 7 Feb. 1782
LUCY HOBBS, m.3, 21 Oct.
1784 **PERNA JUDKINS.**
221. **ANNA**, b. 1759, md. 29 May
1777 **NATHANIEL MARDEN.**
222. **HANNAH**, b. 1762, d. 23 Dec.
1843 at Epsom, md. 17
Sep. 1780 **WILLIAM YEATON**
223. **ELIZABETH**, b. 1764, d. unmd
1835.
224. **JOSEPH**, b. 1766, md. 25
Dec. 1781 **SALLY WALLIS.**
225. **BENJAMIN**, b. 1769, md.
BETSY WOODS.
226. **SALLY**, b. 1776 at Epsom,
md. 16 Nov. 1797 **LEMUEL
BUNKER.**

98. **LEVI TOWLE** [JONATHAN 42] He was born 22
Sep. 1731. He married 11 Oct. 1753 **RUTH
MARDEN**. Possibly had a son JONATHAN, b.
1754?

Children: 227. **SARAH**, b. 15 Feb. 1756.
228. **JEREMIAH**, b. 27 Aug. 1758.
229. **JOSEPH**, b. 1 Feb. 1761.
230. **BETTY**, b. 17 July 1763.
231. **ANNA**, b. 21 Sep. 1766.

100. **SAMUEL TOWLE** [JONATHAN 42] He was born 5
Nov. 1735. He married first 21 Aug. 1760

RACHEL ELKINS. He married second ESTHER
JOHNSON. Children by 2nd wife.

Children: 232. OLLY, b. 1763, md. _____ HAM
         233. SARAH, b. 1765.
         234. MOLLY, b. 1767.
         235. JOB, b. 1770.
         236. ESTHER, b. 1772.
         237. DOLLY, b. 1774.
         238. NABBY, b. 1778.

101. JAMES TOWLE [JONATHAN 42] He was born 28
Oct. 1737. His wife is unknown.

Children: 239. JAMES,
         240. JOHN,

103. NATHAN TOWLE [JONATHAN 42] He was born 29
May 1745. His wife is unknown.

Children: 241. LUCY, b. 1767.
         242. NATHAN, b.1771
         243. JONATHAN, b. 17__

106. JOSEPH TOWLE [AMOS 44] He was born 7 Feb.
1747 and died 1 April 1820. He married in
1769 ELIZABETH COFFIN. Settled Porter, Me.

Children: 244. AMOS, b. 1 Oct. 1770.
         245. JOSEPH, b. 3 Sep. 1772.
         246. WILLIAM,
         247. EZRA, b. 14 Feb. 1776, md.
             31 Mar. 1831 REBECCA
             FRENCH.
         248. NANCY, b. 24 Apr. 1778.
         249. DANIEL, b. 24 Jan. 1780,
             md. 6 Jan. 1808 POLLY
             LADD ?
         250. ELIZABETH, b. 27 Apr. 1783.
         251. SARAH, b. 26 Mar. 1785, md.
             22 Aug. 1803 SAMUEL
             TAYLOR.
         252. DAVID, b. 27 Mar. 1787.
         253. SIMON, b. 16 May 1794.

107. **AMOS TOWLE [AMOS 44]** He was born 6 May
1749 and died 29 Aug. 1825. he married
19 Mar. 1775 **ABIGAIL DOW**, daughter of
Dea. **SAMUEL DOW**. She born 16 Mar. 1750
and died 13 Nov. 1794.

Children: 254. **AMOS**, b. 6 Apr. 1776, d. 7
Apr. 1855, md. **HANNAH
DRAKE**.
255. **SARAH**, b. 22 June 1778, d.
21 Feb. 1852, md. **MOSES
LEAVITT**.

256. **COMFORT**, b. June 1781, d. 4
Aug. 1832, m.1, **DAVID
MARSTON**, m.2, **COTTON W.
MARSTON**.
257. **OLIVER**, b. 2 Mar. 1783, d.
May 1855, md. 21 Apr.
1806 **BETTY LEAVITT**.
258. **DOLLY**, b. 1 Feb. 1785, m.1,
1 Dec. 1806 **JONATHAN
ROBINSON** of North
Hampton, m.2, 7 July 1818
SIMON LEAVITT.
259. **HANNAH**, b. 7 Mar. 1787, d.
29 Aug. 1844, md, **SIMON
N. DEARBORN**.
260. **SIMON**, b. Nov. 1789, d. 25
Apr. 1866, m.1 **LYDIA
LEAVITT**, m.2, **THEODATE
SANBORN**.
261. **ABIGAIL**, b. 3 Dec. 1791, d.
Sep. 1857, md. 27 Sep.
1812 **THOMAS NUDD**.

114. **JACOB TOWLE [BENJAMIN 53]** He was born 16
June 1744. He married _____ **MOULTON**.

Children: 262. **LUCY**,
263. **EBENEZER**,
264. **MARY**,

117. **ELISHA TOWLE [ELISHA 54]** He was born 23
Sep. 1739 and died 7 Jan. 1820. He
married **ANN SANBORN** daughter of **JONATHAN
SANBORN**. She bp 23 Mar. 1740 and died 16
Jan. 1824.

    Children: 265. **MARY**, b. 11 Sep. 1761, d. 3
June 1844, md. 18 Nov.
1787 **JAMES PHILBRICK**, 4
children.
266. **JOSHUA**, b. 20 Oct. 1764,
md. Apr. 1787 **OLIVE
BROWN**.
267. **JEREMIAH**, b. 18 Aug. 1767,
md. **PATTY HARDING** of
Gorham, Me.
268. **SARAH**, b. 9 Apr. 1770, d.
27 Oct. 1858, md.
JONATHAN SEAVEY. Had:
ELEANOR, b. 1779
269. **ELISHA**, b. 2 Feb. 1773, md.
8 Apr. 1797 **SARAH BRAGG**.
270. **PRISCILLA**, b. 20 Oct. 1775,
d. 6 Oct. 1858, md. 5
Nov. 1800 **SAMUEL
PHILBRICK**.
271. **ANN**, b. 6 Apr. 1778, d. 16
Feb. 1857, m.1, **SAMUEL
PALMER**, m.2, **THOMAS P.
MERRILL**. 9 children.
272. **ABNER**, b. 20 Jan. 1781, md.
_____, Res. Gorham, Me.
273. **AARON**, b. 10 Dec. 1789, d.
at sea unmd. 1806.

120. **BENJAMIN TOWLE ELISHA 54]** He was bpt. 8
Dec. 1745. He married **ABIGAIL EDGERLY**
daughter of **JOSEPH EDGERLY**. Res. at
Candia, N.H.

    Children: 274. **SALLY**, b. 2 Sep. 1769.
275. **JOSIAH**, b. 8 Oct. 1770.
276. **NANCY**, b. 18 Dec. 1772.

PHILIP TOWLE, HAMPTON, N.H.

277. ELISHA, b. 12 Mar. 1775.
278. JOSEPH, b. 30 Mar. 1777.
279. MARY, b. 24 Sep. 1781.
280. COMFORT, b. 25 Nov. 1784.
281. NABBY, b. 2 June 1787,

134. PHILIP TOWLE [PHILIP 55] He was born 20
Oct. 1737 and died 19 Mar. 1793. He
married 15 Dec. 1763 ANNA PAGE daughter
of STEPHEN PAGE. She bp 10 Jan. 1746 and
died 7 May 1775. Town Clerk, Selectman
several years. Guardian of child of AMOS
TOWLE, 1 Mar. 1759.

Children: 282. JABEZ, b. 12 Sep. 1764, md.
25 July 1790 ANNA
JOHNSON.
283. ANNA, b. 19 Nov. 1767, d.
20 Oct. 1816 md. 13 Apr.
1784 DANIEL PAGE.
284. PHILIP, b. 5 Apr. 1770,
twin, d. Sep. 1831, md.
16 Aug. 1792 BETTY NUDD
285. LYDIA, b. 5 Apr. 1770,
twin, d. 25 Apr. 1771.
286. LYDIA, b. 22 Feb. 1773, d.
4 May 1843, md. 13 Apr.
1793 DANIEL TOWLE [#194]

140. CALIB TOWLE [CALEB 57] He was born 11
Dec. 1737 at Chester. He married RUTH
PAGE. Res. Danville, N.H.

Children: 287. ABIGAIL, b. 24 Mar. 1761.

142. JEREMIAH TOWLE [CALEB 57] He was born 19
June 1745 at Chester. He married MARY
SARGENT. Res. Danville, N.H.

Children: 288. CALIB, b. 5 Sep. 1766.
289. MOLEY, b. 1 Jan. 1769.
290. SARAH, b. 7 Sep. 1771.
291. REUBEN, b. 14 June 1774,
md. ABIGAIL _____.
292. NICHOLAS, b. 5 May 1777.

293. PHEBE, b. 6 Aug. 1779.
294. JUDITH, b. 6 July 1783.
295. LUCY, b. 13 Mar. 1787.

143. JAMES TOWLE [CALEB 57] He was born 31 Dec. 1747 at Chesterand died 31 Dec. 1825 at Danville, N.H. He married 13 Sep. 1768 ABIGAIL COLBEY at Hampstead. dau. of ENOCH & SARAH (SARGENT) COLBEY. She born 19 Dec. 1749 at Salisbury and died 12 Feb. 1820. Mass. Res. at Danville, N.H.

Children: 296. ELIZABETH, b. 6 Jan. 1770, md. JEREMIAH ELKINS.
297. ESTHER, b. 7 Aug. 1772.
298. JAMES, b. 7 July 1777, md. 6 June 1799 SALLY NASH.
299. NEHEMIAH, b. 1 Mar. 1781, d. 1861, md. ABIGAIL BEAN.
300. ABIGAIL, b. 26 Dec. 1783, twin, d. 13 Jan. 1864.
301. CALIB, b. 26 Dec. 1783, d. 13 Apr. 1859, md. 9 Apr. 1809 ESTHER WEST.
302. JOHN M., b. 19 Dec. 1802.

147. SAMUEL TOWLE [ANTHONY 58] He was born 20 Nov. 1737 and died 1793. He married 19 Mar. 1760 MARY DEARBORN. Res. Chester and Candia, N.H.

Children: 303. EBENEZER, b. 1765.
304. ELIZABETH, b. 29 Sep. 1761.
305. OLIF, b. 1763.
306. THOMAS, b. 18 Apr. 1767, md. SALLY ROBIE.
307. SAMUEL, b. 19 Mar. 1769, md. LYDIA SARGENT.
308. OLLIF, b. 25 Mar. 1771.
309. EBENEZER, b. 17 Mar. 1775.
310. SARAH, b. 14 Feb. 1777.
311. JONATHAN, b. 5 Nov. 1781. d. 1801 at Havana, Cuba.

312. **RICHARD**, b. 15 Oct. 1783,
md. 7 May 1812 **LYDIA**
EMERSON.
313. **POLLY**, b. 29 May 1786.

159. **ISAAC TOWLE** [ZACHARIAH 59] He was born 23
Feb. 1735, bapt. 6 April 1735. and died
August 1791. he married 14 Feb. 1754
ELIZABETH PHILBRICK, daughter of **NATHAN** &
DORCUS (JOHNSON) PHILBRICK. She born 13
May 1730 and died 5 Feb. 1820. She married
second 9 Jan. 1797 **JONATHAN SWAIN** Esq.
Occ. blacksmith. Res. Chester, N.H.

Children: 314. **SIMON**, b. 1759, d. 11 Dec.
1808, md. 1779 **ELEANOR**
HALL.
315. **ANTHONY**, m.1, **SALLY**
McCLELLON, m.2, **NABBY**
EMERSON.
316. **ISAAC**, b. 1771, d. June
1856, m.1, 1792 **ANNE**
PILLSBURY, m.2, **Wid.**
SALLY BUTTERFIELD, m.3,
Mrs. HANNAH SHACKFORD.
317. **ELIZABETH**, b. 1779, d. 25
Nov. 1798, md. 22 Apr.
1779 **SHERBURNE DEARBORN**.

162. **MARY TOWLE** [ZACHARIAH 59] She was born 21
July 1746 and died 9 May 1830 unmarried.
Had illegitimate son.

Child: 318. **AMOS**, bp 8 Sep. 1764, d. 15
Feb. 1855, md. 1 Aug.
1792 **HANNAH PHILBRICK**.

163. **ZACHARIAH TOWLE** [ZACHARIAH 59] He was
born 9 Dec. 1746 and died 28 May 1803.
He married 25 Feb. 1768 **MARY DEARBORN**.
Res. North Hampton.

PHILIP TOWLE, HAMPTON, N.H.

Children: 319. **ANNA**, b. 1 Aug. 1768.
           320. **ABRAHAM**, b. 28 Oct. 1770.
           321. **JONATHAN DEARBORN.**, b. 23
                Jan. 1773.
           322. **SARAH**, b. 22 Aug. 1777.
           323. **JANE**, b. 21 Apr. 1780.
           324. **MOLLEY**, b. c1786.
           325. **SIMON**,
           326. **JONATHAN D.**,

165. **SAMUEL TOWLE [MATTHIAS 60]** He was born
     about 1738 and died 15 Feb. 1796. He
     married 21 Aug. 1760 **RACHEL ELKINS**
     daughter of **JONATHAN ELKINS**. She born
     20 Dec. 1737.

     Children: 327. **ANNA**, md. 13 Aug. 1784
                     DANIEL PAGE.
                328. **CALEB**, b. 1766, d. 1 Oct.
                     1822, He weighed 515 lbs
                     at time of death.
                329. **BRACKETT**, drowned at sea.
                330. **child**, d. 21 Mar. 1771.
                331. **JEREMIAH**, b. 1 May 1771,
                     d. 20 May 1849.
                332. **POLLY**, liv. 1841, md.
                     JONATHAN LANE.
                333. **ZIPPORAH**, b. 5 Feb. 1774,
                     d. 31 Dec. 1850, md.
                     JOHN SHAW.
                334. **JOANNA**, md **JONATHAN M.**
                     AMBROSE.
                335. **RACHEL**, md. **GREENLEAF**
                     AMBROSE.
                336. **BETSY**, b. 1784, d. Dec.
                     1863, md. **ANTHONY EMERY**.

179. **JOSIAH TOWLE [NATHANIEL 64]** He was bpt
     11 Aug. 1745 and died 21 July 1817. He
     married 10 Nov. 1773 **HANNAH TOWLE [#164]**
     daughter of **MATTHIAS TOWLE**. She bpt 23
     Sep. 1753.

Children: 337. MARY, b. Sep. 1774, d. 20
Apr. 1855, md. 29 Mar.
1795 SIMON BLAKE.
338. HULDAH, b. 12 Oct. 1777.
339. JOSIAH, b. Jan. 1780, d.
8 July 1784.
340. LYDIA, b. 3 Apr. 1783, d.
18 Dec. 1849, md. DANIEL
W. LANE, 8 children.

180. JABEZ TOWLE [NATHANIEL 64] He was bpt. 5
April 1747 and died 20 June 1837. He
married 6 Jan. 1778 SARAH GARLAND daughter
of SAMUEL GARLAND. She born 4 Jan. 1754
and died 17 Nov. 1829.

Children: 341. SAMUEL, b. 9 Dec. 1778, d.
20 Dec. 1852, md. FANNY
JENNESS.
342. DANIEL, b. 28 Dec. 1780,
d. unmd. 11 Nov. 1845.
343. NATHANIEL, b. 14 Feb.
1783, md. ESTHER DAVIS.
344. JABEZ, b. 19 Apr. 1785, d.
6 June 1847, md.
ELIZABETH DOW.
345. JONATHAN, b. c1785, d.
unmd. 5 Mar. 183

FIFTH GENERATION

185. JOSHUA TOWLE [JOSHUA 70] He was born
about 1752 and died 13 Sep. 1797. He
married 31 Oct. 1771 JANE DRAKE. Res.
North Hampton.

Children: 346. BETTY, bp 16 May 1773, md.
JOSEPH SAFFORD ?
347. EBENEZER, bp 9 July 1775.
348. JOSHUA, bp 5 May 1782, d.

> 4 Nov. 1835, md. DEBORAH
> NUDD.
> 349. JOHN, bp 19 Sep. 1784, md.
> MARY WATSON?.
> 350. SHUBAEL, bp 12 Feb. 1786,
> drowned 16 Apr. 1787.
> 351. SHUBAEL, bp 21 Aug. 1788.
> 352. ABRAHAM, bp 22 Apr. 1792.

186. WILLIAM TOWLE [EBENEZER 73?] He was born
23 Jan. 1750. He married MIRIAM BURLEY.
Res. Newbury, N.H.

Children: 353. MOLLEY, b. 26 Jan. 1775.
354. WILLIAM, b. 7 Apr. 1776.
355. CALEB, b. 16 Dec. 1777.
356. EDWARD, b. 26 June 1781.
357. JAMES, b. 16 Apr. 1786.
358. JOHN, b. 7 Oct. 1795.

188. EBENEZER TOWLE [EBENEZER 73] He was born
21 Mar. 1756. He married MOLLEY WELLS.
Res. Newbury, N.H.

Children: 359. EBENEZER, b. 6 May 1776.
360. PAUL, b. 28 Apr. 1778,
m.1, BETTY COLBURN, m.2,
POLLY MERRILL.

194. LEMUEL TOWLE Jr.[LEMUEL 80] He was bpt 12
June 1768 and died 5 Aug. 1807. He
married 14 Nov. 1791 ABIGAIL LANE
daughter of WARD LANE. She born 16 Oct.
1774. She married second 21 Sep. 1818
DANIEL LAMPREY.

Children: 361. JOHN,
362. LYDIA, b. 1 July 1794, d.
7 Apr. 1872. Had:
ABIGAIL A., b. 27 May
1827, md. ELISHA M.
LAMPREY.

363. NEWELL, b. 1798, d. 26
Sep. 1871, md. BETSY
REDMAN. No children.
364. MEHITABEL, b. 1801, d. 2
Feb. 1877, md CHARLES W.
CLEMENT.
365. CHARLOTTE, b. c1798, m.1,
JOHN MOULTON, m.2,
REUBEN MARDEN.

195. JOSEPH TOWLE [JOSEPH 83] He was born 1768
and died 11 Oct. 1828. He married 22 Nov.
1790 SARAH MARSTON, daughter of JOHN
MARSTON. She born 7 May 1768 and died 24
Sep. 1843. Occ. carpenter. Kept a store
at Hampton, N.H..

Children: 366. JOHN, b 1791, d. 1 Dec.
1857, md. HANNAH LOCKE.
Had: ELDRIDGE, b. c1818,
HORATIO.
367. SARAH, b. 21 Feb. 1793, d.
1 Mar. 1871, md. 7 Dec.
1815 JONATHAN DEARBORN.
3 sons.
368. MARY, d. 24 July 1870, md.
JOHN STEVENS.
369. child, b/d. Mar. 1796.
370. JOSEPH, b. 11 Mar. 1796, d.
Feb. 1864, md. widow MARY
SANBORN, d/o JAMES TUCK.
371. FREDERIC, b. 1799, d. 18
June 1845, md. BETSY
HARRINGTON.
372. BELINDA, b. c1801, md.
NATHANIEL JENKINS.
373. ELIZABETH, b. c1803, md.
BENJAMIN CLAPP.
374. DARIUS, b. 1805, d. 21 Jan.
1862, md. SALLY DOWNS,
She d. 24 Dec. 1866.
No children.
375. LUTHER,

376. ARCHIBALD EMERY, md. JULIA
STOR.
377. HARRIET ATWOOD, d. 7 Apr.
1847, md. HENRY NOYES.
2 children.

197. DANIEL TOWLE [AMOS 87] He was born 29
Oct. 1767 and died 11 June 1818. He
married 13 Apr. 1793 LYDIA TOWLE [#234]
daughter of Ens. PHILIP TOWLE.

Children: 378. PHILIP, b. 24 July 1793, d.
unmd. 21 July 1816.
379. AMOS, b. 22 Jan. 1796, d.
Oct. 1855, md. POLLY
PERKINS.
380. SALLY, b. 30 Apr. 1798, d.
7 Sep. 1812.
381. DANIEL, b. 12 Jan. 1802,
m.1, MARY VARNEY, m.2,
_____ SNELL.
382. ANNA, b. 22 Dec. 1807, d.
22 Mar. 1852, md. 1835
SIMON S. AMES of Boston.

204. JAMES TOWLE [ABRAHAM P. 94] He was born
26 Nov. 1776 and died 15 June 1859. He
married 15 Aug. 1798 ABIGAIL BROWN
daughter of MOSES BROWN. She born 28
Nov. 1778 and died 17 Mar. 1853.

Children: 383. ABRAHAM PERKINS, b. 17 Sep.
1800, d. 3 June 1879, md.
ELIZA BROWN.
384. JOHN MOULTON, b. 19 Dec.
1802, d. 1890 BETSEY
PINDER.
385. MOSES, b. 12 Sep. 1805, d.
15 Dec. 1890, md.
CHRISTINA BATCHELDER.
386. MARY ANN, b. 1808, d. 14
Mar. 1810.
387. MARY ANN, b. 1 Aug. 1810,
d. 15 Sep. 1844, md. 12
July 1828 JOHN DEARBORN.

388. **NANCY L.**, b. 4 Feb. 1812
        d. 2 Mar. 1881, md. 12
        Apr. 1836 **SEWELL W. DOW.**
389. **OLIVER**, b. 30 Apr. 1815,
        m.1, **ELIZABETH L. WEEKS**,
        m.2, **Mrs. MARY HAINES.**
390. **ELIZA B.**, b. 1 Mar. 1819,
        md. 22 Nov. 1843 **DAVID S.**
        MARSTON.

205. **JAMES TOWLE [JAMES 95]** He was bapt. 3 May
     1766 and died 16 June 1828. He married
     ANNA LANE daughter of **SAMUEL LANE.** She
     born 27 Dec. 1779 and died 25 Nov. 1841.
     age 73 years. Res. at Pittsfield, N.H.

     Children: 391. **MARY**, b. 1799, md. **DAVID**
                    JANVRIN of Hampton Falls.
               392. **JONATHAN**, b. 14 Sep. 1800,
                    d. 1875, md. 1827 **SARAH**
                    LANE. 8 children.
               393. **DOROTHY**, b. 6 Aug. 1803, d.
                    12 June 1867, md. 27 Nov.
                    1828 **REUBEN L. SEAVEY.** 5
                    children.

207. **DAVID TOWLE [JAMES 95]** He was born 15
     July 1771 and died 1 May 1828. Called
     Adjutant. He married 13 Nov. 1798
     ZIPPORAH DEARBORN daughter of **JOHN**
     DEARBORN. She born 15 June 1778 and
     died 23 Oct. 1846. He was a blacksmith.

     Children: 394. **NANCY**, b, 22 Nov. 1799,
                    d.y.
               395. **NANCY**, b. 27 Oct. 1802, d.
                    10 May 1888, md. 10 May
                    1821 **THOMAS MARSTON.** 1 ch
               396. **MAHALA**, b. 9 Sep. 1804, d.
                    28 Oct. 1861, md. **JACOB**
                    DEARBORN. 3 children.
               397. **RUTH HOLT**, b. 4 Feb. 1809,
                    d. 30 Oct. 1838, md.
                    THOMAS PHILBRICK. 1 son.

PNILIP TOWLE, HAMPTON, N.H.

> 398. CLARISSA, b. 22 Feb. 1812,
> d. 2 Nov. 1868, md. DAVID
> M. LEAVITT.

213. JONATHAN TOWLE [JONATHAN 96] He was bapt.
8 June 1777. He married POLLY _____. Res.
Franklin Co., Avon.

> Children: 399. JAMES, b. 26 July 1807.
> 400. JOHN D.. b. 22 Aug. 1809.
> 401. JONATH PARKINS, b. 19 June
> 1811.
> 402. SAMUEL, b. 15 Nov. 1813.
> 403. THEODORE M., b. 13 Nov.
> 1818.

218. SIMON TOWLE [JONATHAN 97] He was born
1753. He married ELIZABETH MARDEN. Res.
Rye, N.H.

> Children: 404. BENJAMIN MARDEN, b. 1782,
> md. BETSY SANBORN.
> 405. SIMON, b. 7 Feb. 1800, d.
> 1872, md. HANNAH YEATON.
> 406. PERNA, b. c1786, d. unmd.
> 407. BETSY, b. c1790, d. 29 Apr.
> 1833, md. 1811 JOHN
> YEATON. 3 ch.

220. LEVI TOWLE, [JONATHAN 97] He was born 1757
He married first MARY LOCKE. He married
second 7 Feb. 1782 LUCY HOBBS and married
third 21 Oct. 1784 PERNA JUDKINS.

> Child by 1st Wife:
> 408. DEARBORN, b. 1783, md.
> RHODA HARVEY.
> by 2bd Wife:
> 409. LEVI GORDON, b. 5 Feb.
> 1785, md. MARY FRENCH.
> 410. PERNA, b. 1788, md. JOHN
> WILSON.
> 411. JOSEPH, b. 4 May 1790, md.
> NANCY RUNDLETT.

PHILIP TOWLE, HAMPTON, N.H.

> 412. GARDNER G., b. 3 Mar. 1791,
>   m.1, ELIZABETH FOGG, m.2,
>   HANNAH ELY.
> 413. PEINNY, b. 18 Oct. 1795?

by 3rd Wife:
> 414. SALLY, b. 11 Sep. 1797,
>   m.1, JAMES RUNDLETT, m.2,
>   ABRAHAM ELY.

224. JOSEPH TOWLE [JONATHAN 97]   He was born
1766. He married 25 Dec. 1781 SALLY
WALLIS. Res. at Epsom, N.H.

Children: 415. HANNAH, d. 30 Apr. 1839,
               md. JONATHAN YEATON. 7 ch
          416. SUSAN, md. SAMUEL GOSS.
          417. SALLY, md. _____ HERSEY.

225. BENJAMIN TOWLE [JONATHAN 97]   He was born
1769. He married BETSY WOODS. Res. at
Epsom, N.H.

Children: 418. JAMES, md. SALLY LAKE.
          419. JONATHAN, md. _____ EMORY.
          420. LEMUEL, md. ANN PRESCOTT.
          421. MARIA, md. _____ LANGLEY.
          422. ELIZABETH.
          423. SALLY, d. unmd.
          424. RHODA,
          425. NANCY, md. JAMES SANBORN.

249. DANIEL TOWLE [JOSEPH 106]   He was born 24
Jan. 1780. He married 6 Jan. 1808 MARY
(POLLY) LADD. Res. Avon, Franklin Co., Me.

Children: 426. JOSES, b. 27 Jan. 1809.
          427. DANIEL, b. 21 Sep. 1810.
          428. HIRAM, b. 22 May 1813, md.
               7 Oct. 1835 BETSY
               WHEELER.
          429. DAVID, b. 8 Feb. 1815.
          430. DAVID, b. 7 Apr. 1817.
          431. MELINDA, b. 16 Aug. 1819.
          432. STEPHEN, b. 21 Oct. 1821.
          433. GEORGE W., b. 6 Oct. 1823.

254. **AMOS TOWLE** [AMOS 107]   He was born April 1776 and died 7 April 1855. He married 13 Nov. 1798 **HANNAH DRAKE** daughter of **JOHN DRAKE**. She born 7 July 1776 and died 28 April 1848.

Children: 434. **MARY**, b. 18 Mar. 1799, d.
                25 Feb. 1867 in Exeter,
                md. **THOMAS LOVERING**. 4
                children.
        435. **DAVID**, b. 28 Feb. 1801, d.
                24 Dec. 1873, md. 17 Apr.
                1823 **MARY GARLAND**.
        436. **JOHN STACY**, b. 13 July
                1803, d. 11 Jan. 1876,
                md. **HANNAH REDMAN**. Had:
                JOHN ALBERT, b. 13 Mar.
                1827.
        437. **OLIVER**, b. 22 Dec. 1808, d.
                30 Jan. 1852 at Exeter,
                md. **ELIZABETH PUSHARD**.
        438. **ELIZABETH**, b. 16 Dec. 1811,
                d. unmd. 4 Sep. 1864.
        439. **ABIGAIL D.**, b. 26 Aug.
                1815, d. 20 Oct. 1856,
                md. **GEORGE W. DRAKE**.

257. **OLIVER TOWLE** [AMOS 107]   He was born 2 Mar. 1782 and died May 1855. He married 21 April 1806 **BETTY LEAVITT**.   Res. Exeter, N.H.

Children: 440. **OLIVER**, b. 16 Dec. 1806,
                d.y.
        441. **MARY G.**, b. 24 Dec. 1807
        442. **OLIVER**, b. 13 Jan. 1810.
        443. **ENOCH W.**, b. 15 June 1811.
        444. **ANGELINE**, b. 4 June 1816.
        445. **BETSEY L.**, b. 22 Nov. 1820.
        446. **AMOS**, b. 23 July 1823.
        447. **ADANIRON J.**, b. 26 June
                1827.
        448. **EMILY B.**, b. 2 June 1829.

260. **SIMON TOWLE** [AMOS 107]   He was born Nov.
1789 and died 25 April 1866.   He married
first 11 Nov. 1813 **LYDIA LEAVITT** daughter
of **JAMES LEAVITT**.   She born 10 Aug. 1792
and died 1 Sep. 1836.   He married second
THEODATE SANBORN daughter of **JEREMIAH
SANBORN**.   She died April 1874 age 68 years
and 8 months.

Children: 449. **ANN BRACKETT LEAVITT**, b. 15
Sep. 1813, d. 4 Apr. 1837
md. June 1831 **JOHN MASON**.
450. **LYDIA MARIA**, b. 7 Jan.
1819, d. 2 June 1839.
451. **JAMES LEAVITT**, b. 26 Mar.
1820, d. 14 Mar. 1823.
452. **SIMON FRANKLIN**, b. 21 Oct.
1821, D. 8 mAR. 1843, md.
8 Feb. 1843 **MARY E.
TARLTON**. She m.2, **SIMON
L. JENNESS**.
453. **ABIGAIL**, b. 21 June 1825,
md. **CHARLES H. COFFIN**.
454. **THOMAS JEFFERSON**, b. 13
July 1827, md. **ELIZABETH
A. BROWN**.

269. **ELISHA TOWLE** [ELISHA 117]   He was born 2
Feb. 1773. He married 8 April 1797 **SALLY
BRAGG** at Salisbury, Mass.   Res.   at
Salisbury.

Children: 455. **ROBERT**, b. 17 July 1797,
md. 8 Jan. 1833 **HANNAH M.
PIKE**.
456. **MARY ANN**, b. 30 Apr. 1799,
md. 3 Apr. 1829 **JAMES P.
BLANCHARD**.
457. **LYDIA**, b. 22 Oct. 1800.
458. **STEPHEN M.**, b. 9 May 1803,
md. 23 Sep. 1823 **SARAH W.
DOLE**.
459. **SOPHIA**, b. 10 Feb. 1806,
md. 18 June 1828 **EDWARD
MORRILL**.

PHILIP TOWLE, HAMPTON, N.H.

  460. **AARON**, b. 22 Aug. 1807.
  461. **SUSAN F.**, b. 9 May 1810,
    md. 7 Jan. 1829 **JOHN**
    FLOYD.
  462. **ALMIRA**, b. 16 Dec. 1813.
  463. **SYDNEY SMITH**, b. 4 Mar.
    1816.
  464. **SARAH JANE**, b. 14 Aug.
    1819.
  465. **FRANCES S.**, b. 14 Nov.
    1821, md. 4 Nov. 1843
    WILLIAM P. NOYES.

282. **JABEZ TOWLE** [PHILIP 134] He was born 12
Sept. 1764. He married 25 July 1790 **ANN
JOHNSON** daughter of **JAMES JOHNSON**. Res.
Personsfield, Me.

 Children: 466. **JABEZ**, b. 1795, md. 1821
      SUSAN WEDGEWOOD.
    467. **JAMES**,
    468. **DAVID**,
    469. **daughter**,

284. **PHILIP TOWLE** [Ens. PHILIP 134] He was
born 5 April 1770 (twin) and died Sept.
1831. He married 16 Aug. 1792 **BETTY
NUDD** daughter of **SIMON NUDD**. She born
28 Feb. 1770 and died Nov. 1857. He
was a Col.

 Children: 470. **SALLY BRACKETT**, b. 30 Nov.
      1792, d. 16 Aug. 1858,
      md. Dr. **GEORGE ODELL** of
      Greenland.
    471. **DAVID**, b. 12 Oct. 1794, d.
      unmd. 19 May 1827.
    472. **NANCY**, b. 13 Feb. 1796, d.
      unmd. 1 Jan. 1876.
      Evangelist Minister.
    473. **PHILIP**, Dr., b. 29 Sep.
      1798, d. 20 May 1832 in
      S.C., md. Wid. **SARAH
      LEAVITT**. Had: **DAVID
      PHILIP.**

PHILIP TOWLE, HAMPTON, N.H.

474. ELIZA HOOK, b. 31 Mar.
1800, d. May 1877, m.1,
GEORGE BERRY, m.2, 1846
Col. JONATHAN MARSTON.
475. SIMON, b. 24 May 1803, d.
17Jan. 1840, md. SARAH
BERRY.
476. MARY, b. 23 Nov. 1805, d.
28 Feb. 1843, md. 18 Sep.
1842 MOSES COLLINS.
477. PATIENCE JANE, b. 28 Feb.
1807, d. 8 Aug. 1886, md.
WILLIARD E. NUDD, 3 ch.
478. LYDIA HALE, b. 1 June 1811,
md. 21 Nov. 1848 HIRAM
WOOD. Had: EDDIE HALE,
1851-1852.

291. REUBEN TOWLE [JEREMIAH 141] He was born
14 June 1774. He had a wife named ABIGAIL.

Children: 479. LUDOVICUS, b. 5 Nov. 1795.
480. NICHOLAS, b. 10 Aug. 1797.
481. LUCINDA, b. 9 Mar. 1800.
482. DORINDA, b. 17 Sep. 1802.

301. CALEB TOWLE [JAMES 143] He was born 26
Dec. 1783 at Kingston, N.H. and died 13
Apr. 1859 at Danville. He married 9 Apr.
1809 ESTHER WEST, dau. of WILkES &
HANNAH (FORSAITH) WEST. She died 3 Jan.
1855. Res. Danville, N.H.

Children: 483. CHARLOTTE, b. 1809, d. 30
July 1827 at Hawke, N.H.
484. CLARINDA, b. 1810, d. 19
Nov. 1890, md. OREN PAGE.
485. Col. JAMES WILLIAM, b. 10
Oct. 1813, d. 18 Aug.
1868, md. 4 June 1837
LUCINDA T. YORK.
486. ABIGAIL, b. 1816, d. 1833.
487. JARIUS, b. 1818, d. 21 Aug.
1890, md. NAOMI T.
DIMOND.

488. CHARLOTTE, b. 1827, d. 26 July 1832.

312. RICHARD TOWLE [SAMUEL 147] He was born 15 Oct. 1783. He married 7 May 1812 LYDIA EMERSON daughter of MOSES EMERSON. Res. at Chester, N.H. Moved to N.Y.

Children: 489. JOHN DEARBORN, b. 14 Mar. 1813.
490. SOPHIA, b. 9 Feb. 1815.

314. SIMON TOWLE [ISAAC 159] He was born 22 May 1759 at Chester. He married 19 May 1779 ELEANOR HALL daughter of NATHANIEL HALL. Moved about 1805 from Chester to Haverhill, Mass. He died there 11 Dec. 1808. Pvt in Rev. War. Later Col. in militia. She died 5 Feb. 1820. Occ. blacksmith.

Children: 491. EDWARD, b. 24 Dec. 1781, d. 31 May 1829.
492. HENRY, b. 19 Aug. 1788, md. SUSAN PIERCE.
493. CHARLES, b. 7 Sep. 1792.
494. ELIZABETH, b. 19 Aug. 1795, md. 17 Nov. 1814 SAMUEL BROOKS. 6 children.
495. FREDERICK, b. 23 Nov. 1798.

315. ANTHONY TOWLE [ISAAC 159] He married first SALLY McCLELLON. She died 1814. He married second NABBY EMERSON.

Children: 496. CARY, d. unmd.
497. SALLY, m.1, BENJAMIN BAKER, m.2, HENRY ROBIE.

316. ISAAC TOWLE [ISAAC 159] He was born 1771 at Chester. He married 1792 ANNE PILLSBURY daughter of ELIJAH PILLSBURY. She died 1814. He married second 29 Mar. 1817 Widow SALLY BUTTERFIELD. She died 1846. He

PHILIP TOWLE, HAMPTON, N.H.

married third **HANNAH SHACKFORD**. Moved
to Francestown. He died June 1856.

341. **SAMUEL TOWLE [JABEZ 180]** He was born 9
Dec. 1778 and died 20 Dec. 1852. He
married 15 July 1823 **FANNY JENNESS**
daughter of **THOMAS JENNESS**. She born 18
May 1800 and died 28 Feb. 1884.

Children: 498. **SARAH A**, b. 26 Feb. 1824.
499. **LYDIA G**, b. 10 May 1826,
md. 7 Dec. 1848 **JOSEPH
JOHNSON**, 3 children.
500. **ELIZA A**, b. 8 Mar. 1829, d.
30 July 1856, md. 2 Feb.
1854 **MOSES HOBBS**.
501. **EMELINE F**, b. 20 Jan. 1831,
d. 9 Oct. 1849 in Lowell,
Mass.
502. **ISABEL A**, b. 28 Nov. 1833,
md. 30 Sep. 1857
NATHANIEL JOHNSON.
503. **MARY E**, b. 24 Feb. 1835,
md. 2 Aug. 1877 **CYRUS S.
JONES** of Rye, No ch.
504. **ABBY J**, b. 24 Nov. 1836,
md. 13 July 1863 **CHARLES
W. JONES** of Rye. Had:
FANNIE ESTHER, b. 1872.
505. **SAMUEL A.**, b. 14 Oct. 1838,
d. 17 July 1904, m.1, 24
May 1882 **Mrs. MARTHA J.
LEIGHTON**. No children.
m.2, 10 Oct. 1895 **JESSIE
K. GREY**.

343. **NATHANIEL TOWLE [JABEZ 180]** He was born 14
Feb. 1783. He married 6 Aug. 1807 **ESTHER
DAVIS**. Res. Newburyport, Mass.

Children: 506. **SARAH GARLAND**, b. 16 July
1808.
507. **ELIZABETH**, b. 13 Feb. 1810.
508. **NATHAN**, b. 14 Aug. 1813.

509. **THOMAS**, b. 14 Aug. 1813.
510. **HARRIET**, b. 27 Feb. 1821.

344. **JABEZ TOWLE [JABEZ 180]** he was born 19 April 1785 and died 6 June 1849. He married 16 May 1810 **ELIZABETH DOW** daughter of **JOHN DOW**. She born 10 July 1789 and died 21 Jan. 1873. Res. Newburyport, Mass.

Children: 511. **CHARLES LEWIS**, d.y.
512. **CHARLES**, d.y.
513. **SAMUEL FREDERICK**, b. 7 Sep. 1814, md. 1 Nov. 1838 **PAMELIA ANN JONES**, d. Denver, Colo. c1890. Had: **MARY ELLEN**, d.y; **OLIVE ANN**. Occ. Carp.
514. **JOHN DOW**, d. ae 20 yrs.
515. **ANTHONY**, b. 15 June 1819, Silversmith, md. 30 Oct. 1841 **HANNAH JONES**. Had: **EDWARD BASS**, b. 24 Dec. 1843, **HANNAH FLORANCE** b. 27 Mar. 1848 & **WILLIAM**.
516. **ELIZABETH FRANCES**, b. 19 Feb. 1821, md. **JOSIAH D. MACE**. 4 children.

SIXTH GENERATION

348. **JOSHUA TOWLE [JOSHUA 185]** He was born 5 May 1782 and died 4 Nov. 1835. He married **DEBORAH NUDD** daughter of **JOHN NUDD** of North Hampton. She born 15 June 1777 and died 22 Sep. 1867.

Children: 517. **ELIZABETH**, md. **GEORGE DANIELS**.
518. **ABRAHAM**, b. 2 Mar. 1810, d. unmd. 3 Sep. 1885.

PHILIP TOWLE, HAMPTON, N.H.

519. RUTH, b. 1815, d Nov. 1870,
md. THOMAS I. BATCHELDER.
520. JOHN, unmd.
521. NANCY, b. 1819, d. 9 Aug.
1851, md. WILLIAM THAYER
of Boston.

349. JOHN TOWLE [JOSHUA 185] He was bpt. 19
Sept. 1784. He married MARY WATSON. Res.
at Hanover, N.H.

Children: 522. DAVID, b. 1807.
523. MARTHA JANE, b. c1810.
524. JOHN R., b. c1815.
525. SARAH, b. 13 Aug. 1822.
526. ELSINA A., b. 4 Oct. 1825.

360. PAUL TOWLE [EBENEZER 188] He was born 28
April 1778. He married first BETTY
COLBURN. He married second POLLY MERRILL.

Children by 1st Wife:
527. AMBROSE, b. 12 Apr. 1800.
by 2nd Wife:
528. TIMOTHY, b. 19 Oct. 1806.

379. AMOS TOWLE [DANIEL 197] He was born 22
Jan. 1796 and died Oct 1855. He married
POLLY PERKINS daughter of JOHN PERKINS.
She born 26 July 1794 and died 24 Jan.
1883. Occ. carpenter, trader, had hotel
at Boars Head 1819, sold 1822. Res.
Stafford.

Children: 529. RUTH ANN, b. 12 July 1826,
md. LEMUEL BUNKER of Rye.
530. ABRAHAM B, b. 12 Dec. 1828,
md. 6 May 1858 LUCRETIA
J. JOHNSON. She d. 15
Mar. 1881. Had: HERBERT
J., b. 1859; MARCUS E.,
b. 1861; JEREMIAH, b.
1862; ALBERT W., b. 1864;

PHILIP TOWLE, HAMPTON, N.H.

ANNIE S., b. 1865; GEORGE
H., b. 1871.

385. MOSES TOWLE [JAMES 204] He was born 12
Sept. 1805 and died 15 Oct. 1890. He
married CHRISTINA BATCHELDER. She died
2 June 1890.

Children: 531. MARY ANN, b. 29 Nov. 1845,
md. 23 Mar. 1870 EDWIN D.
LAMPREY.
532. SARAH ABBIE, b. 1847.
533. JOHN WESLEY, b. 9 Oct.
1849, md. 1871 MARY M.
GODFREY. Had: ERNEST L.,
b. 1871; ANNIE W., b.
1874.
534. ALGIE B., b. 30 Mar. 1854,
d. unmd. 3 July 1878.
535. CHARLES A., b. 5 Jan. 1856.
536. HENRY W., b 16 Feb. 1860,
md. 22 Aug. 1891 ABBY J.
NASON of Manchester.

389. OLIVER TOWLE [JAMES 204] He was born 30
April 1815. He married first 4 Sep. 1842
ELIZABETH WEEKS. She died 1884. He
married second Sep. 1886 Mrs. MARY
HAINES of Haverhill, Mass. All childen
by 1st wife.

Children: 537. MARY ELLEN, b. 25 Oct.
1843, d. 4 Feb. 1851.
538. JAMES HUBBARD, b. 12 Feb.
1845, md. 12 Aug. 1869
THEODORA EVERETT. Had:
EDWIN, CLARENCE, THOMAS.
539. OLIN CLARK, b. 16 May
1847, md. KATE SMITH,
3 children.
540. OSMAN BAKER, b. 4 Feb.
1852, d. 31 May 1861.
541. MARY E., b. 19 Apr. 1854.
542. LURA ELLA, b. 10 Sep.
1858, d. 10 Aug. 1859.

543. **BENJAMIN FRANKLIN**, b. 21
   Dec. 1860, md. **MILLE**
   _____.

405. **SIMON TOWLE** [SIMON 218] He was born 7
Feb. 1800 and died 1872. He married
HANNAH YEATON. Res. at Epsom, N.H.

Children: 544. **CHARLES AUGUSTUS**, b. 14
   Nov. 1824, d. 21 July
   1830.
   545. **OLIVE S.**, b. 13 June 1827,
   d. 1 July 1830.
   546. **LUCY MARIA**, b. 14 Jan.
   1830, md. **JOSEPH PICKARD**.
   547. **ALVINA ANN**, b. 14 Feb.
   1832, md. **CHARLES
   PICKARD**.
   548. **GARDNER S.**, b. 29 Jan.
   1833, md. **SUSAN
   ROBERTSON**.
   549. **EMELINE Y.**, b. 14 Mar.
   1834, d. 1 Apr. 1887,
   unmd.
   550. **CHARLES Wm**, b. 25 Nov.
   1840, d. 24 Dec. 1899,
   md. **REBECCA TOWLE**.

411. **JOSEPH TOWLE** [LEVI 220] He was born 4 May
1790 at Epping. He married **NANCY RUNDLETT**.
Res. at Epping, N.H.

Children: 551. **GEORGE W.**, b. 19 Sep. 1810.
   552. **CHARLES D.**, b. 9 Dec. 1815.
   553. **JOSEPH WARREN**, b. 15 Aug.
   1825.

412. **GARDNER TOWLE** [LEVI 220] He was born 3
Mar. 1791 at Epping. He married 7 Sep.
1809 at Newbury, Mass. **ELIZABETH
(BETSY) FOGG**. Res. at Lee, N.H. He had
a second wife **HANNAH ELY** at Portsmouth.

Children: 554. **ELIZABETH**, b. 10 Oct. 1811.

555. **MARY A.**, b. 2 Jan. 1814
556. **GEORGE P.**, b. 2 Oct. 1819.
557. **JOHN F.**, b. 21 Apr. 1822.
558. **LEVI**, b. 12 Sep. 1824.
559. **SARAH JOSEPHINE**, b. 3 Oct. 1827.
560. **HAMILTON E.**, b. 24 June 1833.

By 2nd Wife:
561. **HENRY RICHARD**, b. 11 Mar. 1839.

435. **DAVID TOWLE** [AMOS 254] He was born 28 Feb. 1801 and died 24 Dec. 1873. He married 17 Aug. 1823 **MARY GARLAND** daughter of **DAVID GARLAND**. She born 3 May 1805. Carpenter and Undertaker.

Children: 562. **MARY F.**, b. 7 Sep. 1830, md. 19 May 1858 **GEORGE W. LANE**. 4 children.
563. **ANN M.**, b. 10 Mar. 1832, d. Sep. 1859, m.1 **JOHN LYON**, m.2, **Dr. WILLIAM T. MERRILL.**
564. **GEORGE W.**, b. 15 June 1834, md. **HARRIET M. DAVIS**. No children. Carp. & Mach.
565. **CHARLES A.**, b. 9 Dec. 1837, d. 4 July 1856.
566. **SARAH H.**, b. 11 Mar. 1840.
567. **JOSEPH R.**, b. 10 May 1842, md. 27 May 1868 **NELLIE F. BURGER**. No children.
568. **DAVID AMOS**, b. 10 Apr. 1845, md. **ABBY A. DOW**. Had: **MAUDE A.**, b. 1877, d. 1890; **ANNE B.**, b. 1880; **ALICE**, b. 1887.

436. **JOHN STACY TOWLE** [AMOS 254] He was born 13 July 1803 and died 11 Jan. 1876. He married 24 Nov. 1825 **HANNAH REDMAN** daughter of **JOSEPH REDMAN**. She born 12 May 1806 and died 24 Jan. 1888.

Children: 569. JOHN ALBERT, b. 13 Mar.
1827, md. 4 Nov. 1854 ANN
DRAKE. Had: AMOS M., b.
1856; EVERETT S., b.
1858; ANNIE, b. 1863, d.
1864; NELLIE M., b. 1865;
EDWARD B., b. 1866; FRED
G., b. 1871; FLOSSIE B.,
b. 1887.
570. AMOS J., b. 1 Apr. 1828, d.
23 June 1878, md. May
1853 CLARISSA SHAW. Had:
FRANK P., b. 1854; CLARA
M., b. 1859, d. 1870;
HATTIE F., b. 1860;
CARRIE E., b. 1866; ALICE
H., b. 1869.
571. MARIANNA, b. 2 Feb. 1834,
md. 1859 A.D. BROWN. 2
children.

454. THOMAS JEFFERSON TOWLE [SIMON 260] He was
born 13 July 1827. He married 29 Nov. 1854
ELIZABETH ANN BROWN daughter of MOSES
BROWN. She born 1 Sep. 1829 and died 29
Nov. 1854.

Children: 572. ANN MARIE, b. 21 Aug. 1855,
d. 27 Dec. 1868.
573. CHARLES FRANK, b. 2 Dec.
1858, d. unmd. 10 Jan.
1891.
574. GEORGE CLINTON, b. 1 July
1861.
575. SAMUEL FREDERIC, b. 6 June
1866.

458. STEPHEN M. TOWLE [ELISHA 269] He was born
9 May 1803. He married 23 Sep. 1823 SARAH
W. DOLE.

Children: 576. SYRENE WEBSTER, b. 27 June
1832.
577. STEPHEN M., b. 17 June
1834.

466. JABEZ TOWLE [JABEZ 282] He was born 1795.
He married 1821 SUSAN WEDGEWOOD.

Children: 578. JABEZ, b. c1821.
         579. MARY A., b. c1822.
         580. MEHITABLE, b. c1824.
         581. SUSAN, b. c1826.

475. SIMON TOWLE [Col. PHILIP 284] He was born
24 May 1803 and died 17 Jan. 1840. He
married SARAH BERRY of Greenland, N.H. She
died 28 Jan. 1886, ae 77 years.

Children: 582. SIMON PHILIP, b. Feb. 1833,
             d. 27 July 1893, md. 19
             Apr. 1874 Mrs. ELLEN C.
             COLBY.
         583. MARY ELIZABETH, b. Feb.
             1835, d. 1877, md. CYRUS
             H. MILLER.
         584. GEORGIANNA BERRY, b. Feb.
             1837, d. 13 Oct. 1878,
             md. HENRY J. MARGERUM. No
             children.
         585. S. ANGELIA, b. Feb. 1839,
             d. 2 Oct. 1840.

485. Col. JAMES WILLIAM TOWLE [CALEB 301] He
was born 10 Oct. 1813 at Danville, N.H.
and died 18 Aug. 1868 at Chester, N.H.
He married 4 June 1837 LUCINDA T. YORK,
daughter of EZEKIEL & NANCY (FOLSAM)
YORK. She born 10 Jan. 1813 Newbury, Me.
and died 24 Jan. 1894 at Chester, N.H.
She may have had Indian blood. Res. at
Res. at Chester, N.H.

Children: 586. CALEB AUSTIN, b. 24 Nov.
             1841, d. 30 Sep. 1849.
         587. JAMES WILLIAM Jr., b. 20
             July 1851, d. 27 June
             1923, m.1, 14 June 1873
             SARAH JANE BROWN, div.

22 Apr. 1896, m.2, 28
June 1922 **VALERIA A.
LEWIS.** 4 children.

491. **EDWARD TOWLE [SIMON 314]** He was born 25
Dec. 1781 and died 31 May 1829. He
married 25 June 1807 **NANCY ELLIOT** of
Chester. She born 16 June 1785.

Children: 588. **EMILY H.**, b. 10 Mar. 1810,
d.y.
589. **ELIZABETH**, b. 10 Aug. 1812,
md. 15 Nov. 1837 **HIRAM
MORGAN.**
590. **ELEANOR**, b. 28 July 1816.
591. **NANCY E.**, b. 1 Nov. 1818,
md. **GEORGE S. TOWLE.** had:
ADELAIDE.
592. **CHARLES S.**, b. 25 July
1822.

492. **HENRY TOWLE [SIMON 314]** He was born 19
Aug. 1788. He married **SUSAN PIERCE**
daughter of **JAMES PIERCE.**

Children: 593. **ANTONETTE,**
594. **EMILY H.,**

493. **CHARLES TOWLE [SIMON 314]** He was born 7
Sep. 1792 at Chester. He married 14 Jan.
1828 **LUCY BELLOWS.** She born 1 Jan. 1806.

Children: 595. **ELEANOR**, b. 31 Aug. 1828.
596. **CHARLES B.**, b. 13 Mar.
1830, d.y.
597. **EDWARD,**
598. **EMILY**, b. 25 Apr. 1833.
599. **CHARLES E.**, b. 11 May 1837.

505. **SAMUEL A. TOWLE [SAMUEL 341]** He was born
14 Oct. 1838 and died 17 July 1904. He
married first 24 May 1887 **Mrs. MARTHA J.
LEIGHTON.** She died 13 Jan. 1892. He
married second 10 Oct. 1895 **JESSIE K.
GREY.**

PHILIP TOWLE, HAMPTON, N.H.

Children: 600. **FANNIE J.**, b. 1901, md.
            WALTER DRYSDALE.
      601. **SAMUEL A.**, b. 13 Aug. 1904.
           md. 21 June 1930 **MARGARET**
           S. MURREY.

PHILIP TOWLE, HAMPTON, N.H.

ISABELLA AUSTIN FAMILY

1. ISABELLA AUSTIN [FRANCIS 2] She was born
about 1633 possibly at Colchester, Co.
Essex, England. She died at Hampton, N.H.
7 Dec. 1719. She married 19 Nov. 1657
PHILIP TOWLE. She was arrested for
suspicion of witchcraft. A trial held at
Hampton on 7 Sep. 1680 and she was
jailed. She was released the following
year after ISAAC MARSTON and JOHN REDMAN
posted her bail. [see Appendix page 80]
See Philip Towle #15 for their children.

2. FRANCIS AUSTIN. He was born in England
perhaps about 1607. He died before 13
July 1642 when a land grant was made at
Hampton to widow AUSTIN. He married 2
Oct. 1632 at St. Mary the Virgin,
Colchester, Co. Essex, England, ISABEL
SMITH (4). She was the daughter of JOHN
BLAND and ISABEL SMITH. They emigrated
first to Dedham, Mass. before removing
to Hampton, N.H. by 30 June 1640 when he
received a land grant. She married
second by 1644 THOMAS LEAVITT. She died
19 Feb. 1699.

   Children: (1) i. ISABELLA, b. c1633, md.
                     19 Nov. 1657 PHILIP
                     TOWLE, d. 7 Dec. 1719.
                 ii. JEMIMA, bp. 24 Jan. 1641,
                     md. 10 July 1660
                     JOHN KNOWLES.
                iii. KEZIAH, bp. 24 Sep. 1641,
                     md. _____ TUCKER.

3. JOHN BLAND ALIAS SMITH. His mother was
named ADRIAN. His will is dated 12 Nov.
1663. Names wife as JOANNA. First wife
was named ISABEL? An ISABEL SMITH, wife

PHILIP TOWLE, HAMPTON, N.H.

of **JOHN SMITH** died 12 July 1639, aged 60 years. [b. c1579]. On Martha's Vineyard in 1646.

Children: (4) i. ISABEL, b. c1611, md. 2 Oct. 1632 **FRANCIS AUSTIN**.

Note: the relationship between Francis Austin of Hampton and **JOSEPH, MATHIAS, SAMUEL** and **BENJAMIN AUSTIN** of Dover, N.H. is unknown. Francis could have been a brother or perhaps their father, if he had a first wife.

APPENDIX

SUMMARY OF PHILIP TOWLE ENTRIES FOUND
IN Co. DEVON, ENGLAND.

1577 Oct. 19	md.	Philip Tolly - Florance Dow at Winckleigh.
1579/80 Mar. 26	bp.	Zachary, s/o Phillippe Tolly at Lapford.
1591 Nov. 4	bp.	Margaret, d/o Phillippe Tolly at Lapford.
Nov. 22	bur.	Margaret, d/o Phillippe Tolly at Lapford.
1593 Oct. 18	bp.	William, s/o Philip Tolly at Lapford.
1610 June 9	md.	Philip Towell - Margaret Whyte at Crediton.
1612 Dec. 20	bur.	Philip Toly at Lapford.
1623 Feb. 29	bp.	Joan, d/o Philip Tule at Crediton.
1624 Jan. 16	md.	Philip Tule - Elizabeth Baslasyn at Crediton.
1625 May 28	bp.	Joan, d/o Phillip Tule at Crediton.
1626 July 12	bp.	Elizabeth, d/o Phillip Tule at Crediton.
1628 Feb. 6	bp.	Martha, d/o Phillip Tule at Crediton.
Sep. 11	bur.	Martha, d/o Phillip Tule at Crediton.
1629 July 20	bp.	George, s/o Phillip Tule at Crediton.
1631 Apr. 20	bur.	Philip Tule, carpenter at Crediton.
1631	Will	Philip Tuell of Crediton.
1641	-	Philip Towell in Prot. Rolls for Crediton.
1645 May 31	bp.	John, s/o Phillipp Towell & Margaret at Braunton.
1654 Dec. 26	md.	George, s/o Philip & Eliz. Toole - _____ d/o William _____.
1657 July 31	bp.	Richard, s/o Phillip Tuell & Agness at Braunton.
1663 Aug. 31	md.	Phillipe Toole - Arminall Commons at Crediton.

APPENDIX

SUMMARY OF PHILIP TOWLE RECORDS CONT.

1674   -   Philip Tole at Crediton,
                       Devon Hearth Rolls.
1681/2 Feb. 2   bp.   Elizabeth, d/o Phillip
                       Toole Jr. at Crediton.
1684 May 20   bp.   George, s/o Phillip Toole
                       at Crediton.
1684/5 Mar. 1   bur.   Ellenor, wife of Phillip
                       Toole at Crediton.

COMMENTS:

        Review of the above information indicates
that there where at least six men named Philip
Towle living in County Devon. All but one lived
at Crediton and adjacent Lapford. Braunton is
not close to Crediton.

APPENDIX

PARISH REGISTER/BISHOPS TRANSCRIPT:
CREDITON, CO. DEVON.

1561 Dec. 28	bur.	Robertis Whytte, filius Johannis Whytte
1561/2 Mar. 23	bp.	Johes Wyte, son Johis Wyte
1563 Sep. 13	md.	William White & Margaret Shapcote
1564 Oct. 6	bp.	John Whyte
1565 Mar. 18	bur.	Thoma Whyte
1568 Apr. 5	bp.	Cylee Whyte
Apr. 25	md.	Edmond Whyte & Margaret Nucum
Sep. 1	bp.	Margaret Whyte
Nov. 2	bp.	Jone Whyte
1568/9 Feb. 14	md.	Robert Whyte & Joys Busshe
1569 Aug. 2	bp.	Nycolas Whyte
Oct. 17	md.	Philip Whyte & Elyzabeth Jefry
1570 Apr. 28	bp.	Thomas Whyte
1570/1 Jan. 15	md.	John White & Mary Rho
1571 May 11	bur.	Elysabeth Whyte [plague]
June 3	bur.	Thomas Whyte
June 17	bur.	Margaret Whyte
July 6	bur.	Mary Whyter
Aug. 17	bur.	Jane Whyte
1572 June 17	bp.	William Whyte
Sep. 23	bp.	Julyan Whyte
Oct. 25	bur.	Hugh Whyte
Dec. 8	bp.	Thomas Whyte
Dec. 14	md.	John White & Jone How
1573 Oct. 9	bp.	Wylliam White
1573/4 Feb. 2	md.	Jearet Whyte & Ennyn Versath
1574 June 3	bp.	Peter Whyte
1574/5 Feb. 2	md.	Robert Whyte & Smyn Verlegh
1575 Apr. 14	bur.	John Whyte
1576 June 13	bp.	Nicolas Whyte
Sep. 21	bp.	Alice Whyte
Nov. 29	bur.	Rychard Whyte
1576/7 Feb. 23	bp.	Robert Whyte
1578 May 21	bp.	John White

APPENDIX

CREDITON PARISH REGISTER CONT.

	Sep. 17	bp.	Robert White
	Dec. 19	bur.	John White
1579	Apr. 16	bp.	John White

Marriage gap 1580 to 1598.

1580 May 17	bp.	George White
1580/1 Mar. 28	bur.	Edmund Whyte
1582 Dec. 12	bur.	Joan Whyte, widowe
1583 July 26	bur.	George White, son of Robert Whyte
Oct. 3	bp.	Agnes White, dau. of Robert
1585 July 15	bp.	Jules White, son of Robert

Incomplete baptisms 1586 - 1591.

1588 Mar. 27	bur.	Nycholas, son Thomasin White, widow
1589 Aug. 24	bp.	George, son of John White
1590 May 9	bur.	John, son of John White
1591 July 19	bp.	Margaret, dau. of John White
1592 June 3	bp.	Annys, dau. of Johan Whyte & John ____
June 7	bur.	Giles, son of Robert White [plague]
June 8	bur.	Robert White
June 8	bur.	Robert, son of Robert White
June 19	bur.	Joyce White, ye widow late Robert
June 19	bur.	John, son of Robert White, dec'd
July 5	bp.	George, son of CHRIST. TOWELL
Nov. 24	bur.	Joan, dau. of John White of Chapel Down
1593/4 Feb. 19	bur.	Julyan White, wyd.
1595 July 14	bp.	Nathaneell, son of CHRISTOPHER TOWELL
1596 Aug. 12	bur.	Jane, wife of John White

APPENDIX

CREDITON PARISH REGISTER CONT.

1596/7 Jan. 12 bur.   Jane, dau. of John White
                     of Green Turner
1597 Aug. 24   bur.   Annis, the wife of
                     Nycholas White
   Dec. 6   bur.   Robert White
1598/9 Jan. 27 bur.   Nycholas White, a poor man
1599 Apr. 1   bur,   John White, a taylor of
                     the west town
   Apr. 20   md.   Edmund Tucker & Emae White
   Apr. 26   bp.   John, son of **CHRISTOPHER**
                     TOWELL
   Aug. 25   bp.   Elizabeth & George, twins
                     of John White
1599/1600 Jan. 19 bp. Judith, dau. of John
                     White of Chapel Down

Baptisms missing 1600 - 1603.

1600 Oct. 25   md.   John White & Tamsin Leggat
   Nov. 3   md.   Mathew Smith & Emme White
   Dec. 12   md.   Stephen Dres & Johan White
1606 Oct. 5   bp.   **CHRISTOPHER**, son of
                     CHRISTOPHER TOWELL
1610 June 9   md.   **PHILIP TOWELL & MARGARET**
                     WHITE
1611 July 5   bp.   **PETER, son of John Tolle**
   July 6   md.   Phillip Butson & Agnes
                     White
1612 July 9   bur.   John Whyte
   July 17   bp.   Jane, dau. of **PHILIP**
                     TOWILL? (not clear)

Marriages missing 1612 - 1622
Baptisms missing 1612 - 1616 then
  incomplete to 1620.

1622/3 Feb. 29 bp.   **Joan, dau. of John T__le**
1624 Jan. 16   md.   **PHILIP TULE & ELIZABETH**
                     BARLASYN
1625 May 8   md.   **Nathaniel Tule** & Elizabeth
                     Tucker
   Aug. 21   bp.   Gilbte, son of Giles White

APPENDIX

```
1625      Sep. 7    bp.  Richard, son of George
Tule
1625/6 Mar. 13 bp.       Walter, son of John White
1627/8 Jan. 6  bp.       Dorothie, dau. of George
                          Tule
          Feb. 6    bp.  Martha, dau. of PHILIP TULE
1628 July 16    bp.      Judith, dau. of Giles White
          Sep. 11   bur. Martha, dau. of PHILIP TULE
1629 July 26    bp.      George, son of PHILIP TULE
1630 June 16    bp.      Henry, son of John White
          Oct. 15   md.  Elizabeth Tule & Nicholas
                          Richards
1631 Nov. 16    bp.      Charitie, dau. of Robert
                          White
1630/1 Feb. 18 bur.      Thomasine White, widow
1631 Apr. 20    bur.     PHILLIP TULE, carpenter
          May 12    bur. Nathaniel, son of Thos.
                          White
1632 Sep. 19    bp.      Mary, dau. of Thos. White
          Nov. 27   md.  Nathaniel Tule & Elizabeth
                          Tremblitt
1633 Sep. 15    bp.      Susanna, dau. of Nathaniel
                          Tule
          Sep. 29   bp.  Thomas, son of William
                          Towle
1634 Dec. 1     md.      Thomazine White & Clement
                          Pidsleigh
1634/5 Jan. 14 md.       Joan White & Edward Newall
          Feb. 10   bp.  Gertrude, dau. of George
                          Tule
          Mar. 30   bp.  William, son of William
                          White
1635 Apr. 19    bp.      Robert, son of Thos. White
                          & Thamzine his w.
1637 Apr. 24    md.      Siblie White & John Butts
1638 Apr. 7     md.      Joan Thule & Edward Newall
          Apr. 28   bur. Judeth Whyte, wid.
          June 2    bur. John White, carpenter son
1640 May 31     bp.      Margaret, dau. of John
                          White & Margaret wife
1640/1 Mar. 21 bp.       John, son of John Towte &
                          Bridget
```

APPENDIX

1641 Sep. 11	bur.	Margaret Tule, widow
Oct. 28	md.	John White & Marce Trost
Dec. 28	bur.	Dorothie, dau. of Giles White
1642 July 17	bur.	Hugh White, son-in-law to William Strong
Oct. 16	bp.	John, son of John White & Marie
1643 Aug. 20	bur.	Margaret Toale, widow
Oct. 21	md.	Anne Towle & Thomas Mortyner
1643/4 Jan. 28	bp.	Giles, son of John White & Marie
1644 Oct. 12	bur.	Christian, dau. of John White & Marie
1644/5 Feb. 27	bp.	Elizabeth, dau. of John White & Marie
1646 July 10	bur.	Nathaniel Tule, weaver
1648 Apr. 2	bp.	John, son of William Towte & Bridget
1649 Apr. 26	bur.	Elizabeth Tule, widow
1650 Oct. 15	md.	Elizabeth Tule & Nicholas Richards
1651 Apr. 14	bur.	John, son of William Towte
Nov. 9	bur.	Humphries, sonne of Robert White
1653 Apr. 23	bur.	Margaret, dau, of John White
Sep. 23	bp.	Marie, dau. of Henrie White & Susanna
1654 Apr. 19	bur.	William Towte
Nov. 5	bur.	Grace White, wid.
Dec. 26	md.	George Toole, son of Philip & Elizabeth _____ dau. of William

gap 1655 to 1661 in baptisms.
gap 1658 to 1669 in burials

1658 June 11	bur.	Sarah Towt, dau. of Thomas
1662 May 11	bp.	Mary, dau. of Walter White
May 23	bp.	John, son of John White

APPENDIX

CREDITON PARISH REGISTER CONT.

1663 Aug. 31	md.	Phillip Toole & Arminell Commons
1674 July 1	bp.	Mathew Tolley, son of John & ffrancis his w.
1676 Oct. 8	bur.	Mathew Tolly, son of John
1679 May 15	bp.	John Tolly & ffrancis, children of John & ffrancis his wife
1681 Feb. 2	bp.	Elizabeth, dau. of Philip Toole Junier
1683 Oct. 14	bur.	Elizabeth Toole
1684 May 20	bur.	George, son of Philip Toole
1684/5 Mar. 1	bur.	Ellenor, wife of Philip Toole
Mar. 10	bur.	Francis, dau. of john Tolly
1687 Dec. 30	bur.	Elizabeth, wife of George Toole
1695 Apr. 19	bur.	George Toole, weaver
1718/9 Jan. 1	md.	James Towell & Elizabeth Jana
1719 Dec. 25	bp.	Henry Tooll, son of George & Alice
1721 Sep. 15	bp.	Alice Tooll, dau. of George & Alice
1722 Dec. 26	bp.	John Tool, son of George & Alice

APPENDIX

ADJACENT PARISH RECORDS:

WINCKLEIGH 1569-1837;

1569 Nov.	md.	John Tolly & Agnes Hatherly
1577 Oct. 19	md.	Philip Tolly & Florance Dow
1623 Apr. 23	md.	Elinora Tolley & Thomas Osmond

COLEBROOKE 1558-1976;

1566 May 19	md.	Roger Toolie & Joane Taylor
June 12	bp.	John, son of Roger Toolie
1568 Nov. 23	bp.	Edmund, son of Roger Toolie
1569/70 Mar. 11	bp.	Robert, son of Roger Tolie
1584/5 Mar. 18	bp.	Thomasyn, dau. of Roger Tolie
1588 Dec. 4	md.	John Toolie & Joan Kentfall
1597 Sep. 18	bur.	Roger Toolie

LAPFORD 1567-1850;

1572 May 14	bur.	Margaret Tolly
1579 June 12	md.	John Tolly & Tomsine Reymontt
1579/80 Mar. 26	bur.	Zachary, son of Phillippe Tolly
1583/4 Jan. 20	md.	William Tolly & Phillipe Sckoble
1591 Nov. 4	bp.	Margaret, dau. of Phillippe Tolly
Nov. 16	bur.	Margaret, dau. of Phillippe Tolly
1593 Oct. 18	bp.	William, son of Phillip Tolly
1612 Dec. 20	bur.	Philip Tolly
1614 May 3	md.	Marie Tolley & George Ballamey
1614/5 Mar. 5	bur.	Jhon Toolye
1631 Aug. 29	md.	William Tolly & Anne Downe

APPENDIX

LAPFORD CONT.

1635/6 Feb. 1	bur.	Anne, wife of William Tolly
1637 June 10	md.	William Tolly & Eddith Gierd
1643 Apr. 23	bur.	John, son of William Tolly
1664 Apr. 5	bur.	Alce, wife of William Tolly
1670 Jan. 20	bur.	William Tolly

SOUTH TAWTON 1541-1903;

1552/3 Jan. 30	bp.	Egline Tollye, dau. of Hugh
1555 May 8	bp.	Robert Tolleigh, son of Hugh
1557 Sep. 2	bp.	Marye Tollye, dau. of Hugh
1559 Nov. 20	bp.	Henry Tolleigh, son of Hugh
1562 May 8	bp.	Ellen Tolley, dau. of Hugh
1564 Oct. 28	bp.	Simon Tollye, son of Hugh
1566/7 Jan. 17	bp.	Hugh Tollye, son of Hugh
1570 May 4	bur.	Hugh Tolley
1579 Aug. 30	bur.	Johanna Tolley, widow
1580 Oct. 26	md.	Henry Tollye & Mary Weste
1583 Aug. 20	bp.	Alice Tollye, dau. of Henry
1584/5 Mar. 29	bur.	Alice, dau. of Henry Tolley
1589 July 19	md.	John Tolley & Johanna Reddaway
1590 Nov. 17	bur.	Mary, wife of Henry Tolley
Nov. 28	md.	Simon Tolley & Wilmot West
1591 Aug. 9	bur.	Robert, son of Hugh Tollye
1591/2 Mar. 28	bur.	Richard, son of Simon Toolye
1592 Dec. 3	bp.	Margaret, dau. of Simon Tolly
1593/4 Feb. 11	md.	Henry Tolley & Johanna Tapp
1594 Sep. 14	md.	Bartholomew Tolley & Barbara Spivrey
1595 Oct. 9	bp.	Richard, son of Simon Tolly

APPENDIX

SOUTH TAWTON CONT.

1595/6 Feb. 26	bur.	_____, wife of Hugh Tollye
1596 Apr. 24	bur.	Barbara, wife of Bartholomew Tolly of Zeale
May 10	md.	Bartholomew Tolley & Mary Kite
1597/8 Feb. 12	bur.	John Tollye als Wykes of Seely Heade
Mar. 12	bp.	John, son of Henry Tollye
1599 Nov. 20	bp.	Henry, son of henry Tolleigh
1600 Apr. 9	bp.	Elizabeth, dau. of Simon Tollye
1602 Aug. 28	md.	Bartholomew Tolley & Richanda Bush
Sep. 27	md.	Mary Tolley & Bartholomew Martyn
1605 July 30	bur.	Henry Tollie
1616/7 Feb. 13	bur.	Hugh Tolly siner
1618/9 Jan. 31	bur.	Richard Tolly
1621/2 Feb. 27	bur.	John Tolly
1627 Sep. 25	md.	Richard Toily & Margery Northmore
1639 May 1	bur.	Willmot Tolley

SHOBROOKE 1538-1799;

1620 Apr. 7	bur.	Walter Tuly
1668 Apr. 10	bp.	Jane, wifw of Mark & Margaret Tolie
1670 Aug. 27	bur.	Jane, dau. of Mark Tollee
1672 Dec. 17	bp.	Lucye, dau. of Markes & Lucye Toley
1686 May 8	bur.	Marke Tolly

EXETER:

1565/6 Jan. 14	md.	Alse Tolie & Robert Stoyell, St. Paul

APPENDIX

1584 May 4	md.	Richard Towill & Dorothi Jere, St. Kerrian
1590 Nov. 17	md.	Willm Towill & Elizabeth Wills, All Hallows
1610 Sep. 4	bp.	Elizabeth, dau. of Jacob Tolly, St. Mary Step
1611 July 8	md.	Markes Towill & Richord Burrington, All Hallows
1618 Oct. 4	md.	John Tewle & Anne Tralman, Holy Trinity
1620/1 Mar. 23	bp.	John, son of John Tewle, Holy Trinity
1622 July 4	bp.	Francis, dau. of John Towle, Holy Trinity
1623 Apr. 6	bp.	Margaret, dau. of John Towill, St. Thos Apostle
1624 June 28	bp.	Margaret, dau. of Jacobe Tolly, St. Mary Steps
1626 Aug. 4	md.	Natha Towell & Joana Starre, St. Martin
1628 May 29	bp.	Margaret, dau. of Nicolas Tewle, St. Mary Steps
1633 Oct. 5	bp.	Julyon, dau. of John Tewle, Holy Trinity
1634/5 Jan. 10	bp.	Grigory, son of John Towle & Anne, Holy Trinity
1664 Sep. 25	bp.	Charles, son of Thos. Toowill, St. Mary Major
1665 July 9	bp.	Christobell, dau. of John Towill, St. Mary Maj.
1669 July 4	bp.	Sarah, dau. of John Toowell, St. Mary Major
1766 Aug. 8	bp.	Susanna, dau. of Philip Towell, St. Sidwell

APPENDIX

LIST OF INDEX OF TOWLE WILLS COUNTY DEVONSHIRE:
[For Parishes Close to Crediton]

Date	Name	Parish	No.

Principal Registry, Bishop of Exeter Court:

Date	Name	Parish	No.
1552	John Towly	Payngton	107
1593	Roger Tolle		m.t.
1605	Cicilie Tolley	Witheridge	161
1605	Henry Tollye	So. Tawton	178
1620	Robert Tawley	Sanford	136w
1624	Roger Tollet	Down St. Mary	Adm.
1625	Michael Towill	Broadclyst	Will
1631	**Philip Tuell**	Crediton	Will
1636	John Tole	Dunsford	Admin.

Arch. of Barnstable Court:

Date	Name	Parish
1564	Richard Towill	Chawleigh
1598	Alice Tolley	Thelbridge
1621/11/6	Edward Tolley	Thelbridge
1629	James Tolley	Wadford Pyre

Archdeaconry Court of Exeter:

Date	Name	Parish	No.
1588	Thomas Towill	Broad Clyst	c.t.466
1593	Roger Tolle		m.t.
1606	Roger Towille		m.a.
1618	Richard Tolly	So. Tawton	Will
1620	Walter Tulie	Shobrooke	Will
1625	James Tolly	Exeter	Will
1700	Emanuel Towill	So. Tawton	Will

Consistory Court of Exeter:

Date	Name	Parish	No.
1624	Thomas Towill	Broad Clyst	404

Cantebury Wills, London:

Date	Name	Parish	No.
1631/11/26	Michael Towell	Broad Clyst	115

P.C.C.

APPENDIX

Note: During World War 2 the city of Exeter was
bombed by the Germans. All the probate
records were destroyed regretfully. The
Index of Wills survives as do several
will abstract books found at the West
Country Library, Exeter, England.

APPENDIX

ROGER TOWLE
BOSTON, MASS.

ROGER TOWLE, Boston. While no evidence has
been found, he could have been related to PHILIP
TOWLE of Hampton, N.H. The name of ROGER was a
name used by the TOWLEs of the parish of
Crediton, Co. Devon. Roger was convicted 1 Dec.
1640 at the Quarter Court held at Boston for
selling 2 lbs. of gunpower to the Indians. He
was called "Mr. Henry Webb's man." He was
probably an apprentice to Mr. Webb. Roger was
admitted to the First Church of Boston on 23
Apr. 1644 and was named on the list of freeman
under the first charter of the Mass. Colony 29
May 1644. What became of Roger Towle is unknown.
Later in Boston records we find a Richard Towle
paying a tax of 24p in 1674 and a Richard Towle
Jr. taxed in 1688. Their relationship to Roger
Towle is unknown.

Perhaps the Roger Towell, willing to go to
St. Christopher 20 Feb. 1639, is the same man.
He is listed as a suspected pick pocket and
haunter of the Custom House. [Bridewell Records]

ISABEL TOWLE
WITCHCRAFT TRIAL

In July, 1680, a little child of John Godfrey
died, and the old cry of *witchcraft* was raised.
An inquest was held, with twelve solid men of
Hampton for jurers, and a verdict rendered: "We
find grounds for suspicion that the said child
was murdered by witchcraft." Rachel Fuller was
blamed.

APPENDIX

ISABEL TOWLE - WITCHCRAFT TRIAL Cont.

Goody (Isabel) Towle was arraigned about the same time, on a different charge, and both she and Rachel Fuller were committed to prison till the setting of the Hampton Court, Sept. 7, 1680. Then "The Court having heard ye case of Rachel Fuller and Isabel Towle being apprehended and committed upon suspition of witchcraft doe order yt they still containe in prisson till bond be given for their good behaviour of £100 a piece during the Courts pleasure.

John Fuller became bondsman for his wife, and Isaac Marston and John Redman, for Goody Towle. They were discharged at the Dover Court the next year.

Source: Dow, Hist. of Hampton, N.H., p.84-85.

COMMENTS:

Since her husband Philip Towle was living why didn't he post her bond? From his probate records we learn that he wasn't poor. Neither Marston or Redman, who posted the bond, were related to Isabel Towle. So why did they do it? Quite a puzzle.

BIBLIOGRAPHY — ENGLAND

1. <u>Devon Subsidy Rolls 1524-7</u>, THomas L. Stoate, Bristol, (1979)

2. <u>Devon Hearth Tax 1674</u>, Thomas L. Stoate, Bristol, Eng. (1982)

3. <u>Devonshire Wills</u>, Chas. Worthy, 2 vol., London, (1896)

4. <u>Devon Will Abstracts</u>, Olive Moger.

5. <u>Devon Will Abstracts</u>, Sir Oswyn Murrey Collection.

6. Index of Wills & Admon., Proved at Court of Arch. of Barnstable 1563 - 1858.

7. <u>Devon Wills & Admin.</u>, v. 35 Dist. Probate Registry Proved at Court of Principal Registry, Bishop of Exeter, 1559-1799, Edw. A. Fry, B.R.S., ltd, London (1908)

8. <u>Devon Wills & Admin.</u>, v. 46 Consistory Court of Bishop of Exeter 1532-1800, Edw. A. Fry, B.R.S. Ltd., London (1914)

9. <u>Devon Wills</u>, v. 56, Wills at Bodmin, R. M. Glencross, B.R.S. Ltd., London (1929).

10. <u>Devon Protestant Returns 1641</u>, A.J. Howard, Bristol, England 2 vol. (1973). Privately printed.

11. <u>Inquisition Post Mortem</u>, v.24 & v.26, Public Record Office, London, New York (1963)

12. <u>Devon Feet of Fines</u>, v.1, 1196-1272; v.2, 1272-1369, Devon & Cornwall Record Society.

13. <u>Visitations of Co. Devon 1564</u>, Frederic T. Colby, Exeter, England (1881).

14. Visitations of Co. Devon 1620, Frederic T. Colby, London, (1872), Harleaun Soc. Publ. v.6.

15. Devon & Cornwall Record Society, v.1 thru v.22, Exeter, Eng. (1906 -   )

16. Devon Parish Marriages, William P. Phillimore, 2 v. (1909-15)

17. Genealogical Gleanings In England, Henry F. Waters, 2 vol., Boston, (1901)

18. Devon Muster Roll for 1569, A,J, Howard & T.L. Stoate, Bristol, England (1977).

19. Devon Record Office, Exeter, England Misc. Crediton Records:

    A3 Tithe Receipts & Misc Payments 1582-1583.
    A11 86 Leases of Tithes of Crediton, Sanford & Exmouth, 1585-1608.
    A13 Tithe Rental 1594, (30 folios)
    A16 Dish. of Charity monies, 1586-1611.
    B219 Acc't Book, Tithe Rec., 1600-1.

20. Parish Registers/Bishop Transcripts of:

Crediton	South Tawton	Woodbury
Exeter	Colebrooke	Newton St. Cyres
Ugborough	Stoke in Teighead	Buckland
Sanford	Witheridge	Modbury
Hatheridge	Lapford	Winckleigh
Sidmouth	Barnstable	Shobrooke
Paignton	Kenn	Sprayton

BIBLIOGRAPHY
NEW ENGLAND

1. History of The Town of Hampton, N.H., Joseph Dow, Salen, Mass. (1893)

2. History of The Town of Rye, N.H., Langdon B. Parson, Concord, N.H. (1905).

3. Samuel Towle Manuscript Collection, (1877) at Newberry Library, Chicago, Ill. [Ref. MS fE7.T6603]

4. NEHGR v.43, p.364, Desc. of Philip Towle, Mrs. A. Lindsey (1889)

5. A Genealogical Dictionary of the First Settlers of New England, James A. Savage, Boston, Mass. 4 vol. (1860-2)

6. NEHGR, V.1, V.2, V.3, V.6, V.7, V.8, V.9, V.10, V.12, V.17, V.18, V.27, V.28, V.29, V.31, V.35, V.41, V.43

AUTHORS BIOGRAPHY

WILLIAM HASLET JONES, has done extemsive English genealogical research in orignial records at the Public Record Office, London, England and at the County Record Offices of; Cumberland, Devon, Essex, Northamptonshire, Hertfordshire, Lancastershire, Norfolk, Shropshire, Warwickshire and Westmoreland, with additional studies conducted at various English libraries including: Society of Genealogists and St. Catherine's House in London, at the West County Studies library, Exeter, at the Norwich City library, etc.

The results from his English research have been published in the NEHGR REGISTER, and included in two books; John B. Threlfall's ENGLISH ORIGINS OF 50 EARLY NEW ENGLAND FOUNDERS, (1990), and in HISTORY OF THE TOWN OF HAMPTON, N.H. (1989), in connection with their 350th anniversary.

Mr. Jones has conducted North American research at the National Archives and at the Library of Congress in Washington, D.C.; at the State Archives of: Arkansas, Illinois, Kansas, Maine, Missouri, New Hampshire, Tennessee and Wisconsin; at State Historical Society Libraries in these States; and at various public and private libraies including the D.A.R. library, Washington, D.C., the Newberry Library, Chicago, Ill., The Southern Baptist Library, Nashville, Tenn., The NEHGS Library, Boston, Mass., the Allen County Library, Ft. Wayne, Ind., the Chattanooga Public library, McGhee-Lawson Library, Knoxville, Tenn. and the Family History Ceneter library. Additional research was conducted at more than 40 County Court Houses in the above named states.

Mr. Jones has served for many years as a volunteer librarian at the Naperville, Illinois branch library of the Family History Center of the Church of Jesus Christ of Later Day Saints.

FINAL THOUGHTS

The English records do not prove with any certainty that Philip Towle of Hampton, N.H. came from the parish of Crediton in County Devon, England. Circumstantial evidence does support this theory. There was a young man named Philip Towle last named in 1641 at Crediton. No marriage or death entry was found in the parish register for Crediton or for any of the adjacent parishes. He certainly could have emigrated to New England. Perhaps he took care of his stepmother and wasn't free to leave until after her death in 1649.

A review of all TOWLE names found in England, for the time period prior to 1700, as found in the Morman International Genealogical Index for 1993, showed that 82 % resided in County Devon. The name of Philip Towle only appeared in Devon and primarily in the Crediton area some 26 times. Logic says that this is where Philip Towle of Hampton probably came from. Regretfully the 1631 will of Philip Towle of Crediton was lost during World War 2. It would have helped to resolve the question.

The question remains; why did Philip Towle come to New England and to Hampton, N.H. in particular? If Roger Towle of early Boston, Mass. was a brother or close relative, that could explain why he came to New England. Can we find any connection between Crediton and New England? Yes we can. Rev. William Cook was the vicar at Crediton from 1595 till his death in 1615. [Most likely he married Philip Towell and Margaret Whyte in 1610] Rev. Cook married in 1597 Martha Whyte the daughter of John Whyte of Standon St. John in Oxford. Was there a possible family connection between the Whytes of Crediton and Oxford? I found none, but we can't rule it out. Rev. Cook had a daughter Elizabeth born about 1602 at Crediton. She married in 1627 William Walton. They later emigrated to Marblehead, Mass. Thus there a is possible

FINAL THOUGHTS CONT.

connection between Crediton and New England.
[See NEHGR v.188, p. 361-8]

On the negative side we do not find any
commonality between the given names used at
Hampton and those used at Crediton. Only 25 %
agreement was found. But we note that all the
names used by Philip Towle of Hampton were
biblical names! This may explain the
differences.

We don't know the occupation of Philip Towle
named in 1641 at Crediton. His father was a
carpenter, so most likely he followed the same
trade. From Hampton, N.H. records it appears
that Philip Towle was a farmer, but he may have
also been a carpenter.

William Haslet Jones

INDEX OF TOWLE NAMES

No.	Name	Birth	No.	Name	Birth
273	Aaron	1789	449	Ann B.L.	1813
460	Aaron	1807	563	Ann M.	1832
504	Abby J.	1836	572	Ann M.	1855
47	Abigail	1699	136	Anna	1728
72	Abigail	1721	92	Anna	1733
77	Abigail	1725	102	Anna	1741
85	Abigail	1735	221	Anna	1759
112	Abigail	1737	231	Anna	1766
118	Abigail	1741	283	Anna	1767
287	Abigail	1761	201	Anna	1768
203	Abigail	1774	319	Anna	1768
300	Abigail	1783	327	Anne	1784
261	Abigail	1791	382	Anne	1807
439	Abigail D.	1815	17	Anne	c1620
486	Abigail	1816	119	Anne	1743
453	Abigail	1825	58	Anthony	1703
272	Abner	1781	155	Anthony	1752
65	Abraham	1719	315	Anthony	_____
156	Abraham	1728	515	Anthony	_____
158	Abraham	1732	593	Antonette	_____
94	Abraham P.	1740	376	Archibald E.	___
320	Abraham	1770			
217	Abraham P.	1788			
352	Abraham	1792	372	Belinda	c1801
383	Abraham P.	1800	31	Benjamin	1669
518	Abraham	1810	52	Benjamin	1711
530	Abraham B.	1828	53	Benjamin	1713
447	Adaniron J.	1827	133	Benjamin	1735
534	Algie B.	1854	120	Benjamin	1745
462	Almira	1813	116	Benjamin	1749
547	Alvina Ann	1832	225	Benjamin	1769
527	Ambrose	1800	404	Benjamin M.	1782
44	Amos	1711	543	Benjamin F.	1860
87	Amos	1740	199	Betsey	1783
107	Amos	1749	336	Betsy	1784
318	Amos	1764	407	Betsy	c1790
244	Amos	1770	445	Betsey L.	1820
254	Amos	1776	230	Bettey	1763
379	Amos	1796	196	Betty	1764
446	Amos	1823	346	Betty	1773
570	Amos J.	1828	199	Bettey	1783
444	Angeline	1816	151	Brackett	1746
271	Ann	1778	329	Brackett	_____

INDEX OF TOWLE NAMES CONT.

No.	Name	Birth	No.	Name	Birth
176	Elizabeth	1741	551	George W.	1815
304	Elizabeth	1761	556	George P.	1819
223	Elizabeth	1764	433	George W.	1823
296	Elizabeth	1770	564	George W.	1834
317	Elizabeth	1779	574	George C.	1861
250	Elizabeth	1783	584	Georgianna	1837
496	Elizabeth	1795			
422	Elizabeth	____			
373	Elizabeth	1803	560	Hamilton E.	1833
507	Elizabeth	1810	35	Hannah	1690
438	Elizabeth	1811	63	Hannah	1714
554	Elizabeth	1811	69	Hannah	1718
589	Elizabeth	1812	74	Hannah	1727
516	Elizabeth	1821	110	Hannah	1735
517	Elizabeth	____	174	Hannah	1739
526	Elsina A.	1825	109	Hannah	1753
501	Emeline F.	1831	167	Hannah	1753
549	Emeline Y.	1834	222	Hannah	1762
588	Emily H.	1810	200	Hannah	1764
594	Emily H.	____	259	Hannah	1787
448	Emily B.	1829	415	Hannah	____
598	Emily	1833	510	Harriet	1821
443	Enoch W.	1811	377	Harriet A.	1847
132	Esther	1734	50	Hebzibah	1706
236	Esther	1772	492	Henry	1788
297	Esther	1772	561	Henry R.	1839
131	Ezekiel	1731	536	Henry W.	1860
247	Ezra	1776	428	Hiram	1813
			93	Huldah	1735
			178	Huldah	1744
600	Fannie J.	1901	182	Huldah	1751
32	Francis	1671	212	Huldah	1775
62	Francis	1711	338	Huldah	1777
169	Francis	c1740			
465	Francis S.	1821			
371	Frederic	1799	159	Isaac	1735
495	Frederick	1798	316	Isaac	1771
			502	Isabel A.	1833
412	Gardner G.	1791			
548	Gardner S.	1833	128	Jabez	1724
10	George	1592	180	Jabez	1747
21	George	1629	282	Jabez	1764

No.	Name	Birth	No.	Name	Birth
278	Joseph	1777	457	Lydia	1800
411	Joseph	1790	478	Lydia H.	1811
370	Joseph	1796	450	Lydia maria	1819
553	Joseph W.	1825	499	Lydia G.	1826
567	Joseph R.	1842			
426	Joses	1809			
28	Joshua	1663	396	Mahala	1804
36	Joshua	c1692	7	Margaret	1579
68	Joshua	1716	421	Maria	____
70	Joshua	1719	144	Mariah	1751
185	Joshua	c1752	571	Marianna	1834
187	Joshua	1753	20	Martha	1627
126	Joshua	1758	48	Martha	c1701
266	Joshua	1764	523	Martha Jane	c1810
348	Joshua	1782	29	Mary	1665
71	Josiah	1721	45	Mary	1695
179	Josiah	1745	41	Mary	1701
275	Josiah	1770	90	Mary	1728
339	Josiah	1780	138	Mary	1732
294	Judith	1782	86	Mary	1737
			173	Mary	1742
			162	Mary/Marah	1746
80	Lemuel	1737	122	Mary	1749
194	Lemuel	1768	154	Mary	1750
420	Lemuel	____	219	Mary	1755
98	Levi	1731	264	Mary	____
220	Levi	1757	265	Mary	1761
409	Levi G.	1785	337	Mary	1774
558	Levi	1824	279	Mary	1781
241	Lucy	1767	368	Mary	____
262	Lucy	____	391	Mary	1799
295	Lucy	1787	434	Mary	1799
546	Lucy M.	1830	456	Mary Ann	1799
481	Lucinda	1800	476	Mary	1805
479	Ludovicus	1795	386	Mary Ann	1808
542	Lura Ellen	1858	387	Mary Ann	1810
375	Luther	____	555	Mary A.	1814
184	Lydia	1755	579	Mary Ann	c1822
192	Lydia	1757	531	Mary Ann	1845
285	Lydia	1770	503	Mary E.	1835
286	Lydia	1773	583	Mary Eliz.	1835
340	Lydia	1783	537	Mary Ellen	1843
362	Lydia	1794	541	Mary E.	1854

No.	Name	Birth	No.	Name	Birth
562	Mary F.	1830	305	Olif	1763
441	Mary G.	1807	539	Olin Clark	1847
60	Matthias	1707	306	Ollif	1771
164	Matthias		232	Olly	1763
150	Maurice	1743	545	Olive S.	1827
43	Mehitabel	1706	257	Oliver	1783
91	Mehitabel	1730	440	Oliver	1806
79	Mehitabel	1732	437	Oliver	1808
364	Mehitabel	1801	442	Oliver	1810
580	Mehitabel	c1824	389	Oliver	1815
431	Melinda	1819	540	Osman B.	1852
234	Molly	1767			
289	Moley	1769			
202	Molly	1772	48	Patience	1704
211	Molly	1774	135	Patience	1740
353	Molley	1775	113	Patience	1741
324	Molley	c1786	477	Patience J.	1807
385	Moses	1805	189	Paul	1756
			360	Paul	1778
			413	Peinny	1795
238	Nabby	1778	208	Perkins	1773
281	Nabby	1787	406	Perna	c1786
276	Nancy	1772	410	Perna	1788
248	Nancy	1778	293	Phebe	1779
472	Nancy	1796	9	Philip	c1590
394	Nancy	1799	15	Philip	c1616
395	Nancy	1802	26	Philip	1659
388	Nancy L.	1812	55	Philip	1698
425	Nancy		129	Philip	1727
591	Nancy E.	1818	134	Philip	1737
521	Nancy	1819	284	Philip	1770
103	Nathan	1745	378	Philip	1793
242	Nathan	1771	473	Philip	1798
508	Nathan	1813	149	Phineas	1742
12	Nathaniel	1595	312	Polly	1786
64	Nathaniel	1716	332	Polly	
343	Nathaniel	1783	270	Priscilla	1775
299	Nehemiah	1781			
363	Newell	1792			
292	Nicholas	1777	335	Rachel	
480	Nicholas	1797	146	Reuben	1735
			291	Reuben	1774
			424	Rhoda	

No.	Name	Birth	No.	Name	Birth
6	Richard	c1571	227	Sarah	1756
312	Richard	1783	233	Sarah	1765
4	Robert	1569	268	Sarah	1770
105	Robert	1744	290	Sarah	1771
455	Robert	1797	310	Sarah	1777
1	Roger	c1545	322	Sarah	1777
16	Roger	c1618	255	Sarah	1778
397	Ruth holt	1809	251	Sarah	1785
519	Ruth	1815	367	Sarah	1793
529	Ruth Ann	1826	506	Sarah G.	1808
			464	Sarah Jane	1819
			525	Sarah	1822
585	S. Angelia	1839	498	Sarah A.	1824
274	Sally	1769	559	Sarah J.	1827
198	Sally	1774	566	Sarah H.	1840
226	Sally	1776	532	Sarah A.	1847
216	Sally	c1784	350	Shubael	1786
470	Sally B.	1792	351	Shubael	1788
414	Sally	1797	161	Simon	1740
380	Sally	1798	190	Simon	1745
417	Sally	____	153	Simon	1749
423	Sally	____	108	Simon	1751
497	Sally	____	218	Simon	1753
66	Samuel	1722	314	Simon	1759
100	Samuel	1735	210	Simon	1779
147	Samuel	1737	260	Simon	1789
165	Samuel	c1738	252	Simon	1794
307	Samuel	1769	325	Simon	____
341	Samuel	1778	405	Simon	1800
402	Samuel	1813	475	Simon	1803
513	Samuel F.	1814	452	Simon F.	1821
505	Samuel A.	1838	582	Simon P.	1821
575	Samuel F.	1866	459	Sophia	1806
601	Samuel A.	1904	490	Sophia	1815
37	Sarah	c1689	458	Stephen M.	1803
51	Sarah	1709	432	Stephen	1821
75	Sarah	1732	577	Stephen M.	1834
84	Sarah	1733	416	Susan	____
111	Sarah	1737	581	Susan	c1826
104	Sarah	1742	461	Susan F.	1810
122	Sarah	1747	463	Sydney S.	1816
152	Sarah	1749	576	Syrene W.	1832
125	Sarah	1756			

INDEX OF OTHER NAMES

INDEX OF OTHER NAMES CONT.

www.ingramcontent.com/pod-product-compliance
Lightning Source LLC
Chambersburg PA
CBHW052048270326
41931CB00012B/2681